MEL BAY'S
FIDDLING
CHORD BOOK

by Craig Duncan

1 2 3 4 5 6 7 8 9 0

© 1992 BY MEL BAY PUBLICATIONS, INC., PACIFIC, MO.
INTERNATIONAL COPYRIGHT SECURED. ALL RIGHTS RESERVED. PRINTED IN U.S.A.

Introduction

This book contains basic chords for practical use on the fiddle. The term *chord* generally refers to a combination of three or more notes. For the purposes of this book, combinations of two or more of the notes in a given chord will be considered as the chord.

The notes of each chord are presented at the top of the page. Then the double and triple stops fall in order from the lowest (notes on the G string) to the highest. The double and triple stops presented have generally been limited to first position. It is best to practice the top line of the page to become familiar with how the notes lie on the fiddle. The double stops should be memorized.

Some chords may have enharmonic names or spellings (ex. F♯ or G♭). If you cannot find the chord you need, check for an enharmonic spelling. Also, in the diminished and augmented chords, the enharmonic spelling is often used to make the notes easier to read.

There are chords that this book does not include such as 9ths, 11ths, 13ths, and half diminished. However, the chords found here are the most frequently used and will cover practically every fiddling situation. Sixth chords have been included because of their prominence in Western swing. The sixth and seventh chords include only the double stops which contain the sixth or seventh.

Many of the voicings found in the book are better than others in different musical contexts. Study and experiment with the chords to determine what works best for you.

Contents

Major Chords
G Major 4
A♭ Major 5
A Major 6
B♭ Major 7
B Major 8
C Major 9
D♭ Major 10
D Major 11
E♭ Major 12
E Major 13
F Major 14
F♯ Major 15

Minor Chords
G Minor 16
G♯ Minor 17
A Minor 18
B♭ Minor 19
B Minor 20
C Minor 21
C♯ Minor 22
D Minor 23
D♯ Minor 24
E Minor 25
F Minor 26
F♯ Minor 27

Diminished Chords
G Diminished 28
G♯ Diminished 29
A Diminished 30
A♯ (B♭) Diminished 28
B Diminished 29
C Diminished 30
C♯ Diminished 28
D Diminished 29
D♯ Diminished 30
E Diminished 28
F Diminished 29
F♯ Diminished 30

Augmented Chords
G Augmented 31
A♭ Augmented 32
A Augmented 33
B♭ Augmented 34
B Augmented 31
C Augmented 32

C♯ Augmented 33
D Augmented 34
E♭ Augmented 31
E Augmented 32
F Augmented 33
F♯ Augmented 34

Seventh Chords
G7 35
A♭7 36
A7 37
B♭7 38
B7 39
C7 40
C♯7 41
D7 42
E♭7 43
E7 44
F7 45
F♯7 46

Minor Seventh Chords
Gm7 47
G♯m7 48
Am7 49
B♭m7 50
Bm7 51
Cm7 52
C♯m7 53
Dm7 54
E♭m7 55
Em7 56
Fm7 57
F♯m7 58

Sixth Chords
G6 59
A♭6 60
A6 61
B♭6 62
B6 63
C6 64
C♯6 65
D6 66
E♭6 67
E6 68
F6 69
F♯6 70

The G Chord

The notes in the G chord are G, B and D.

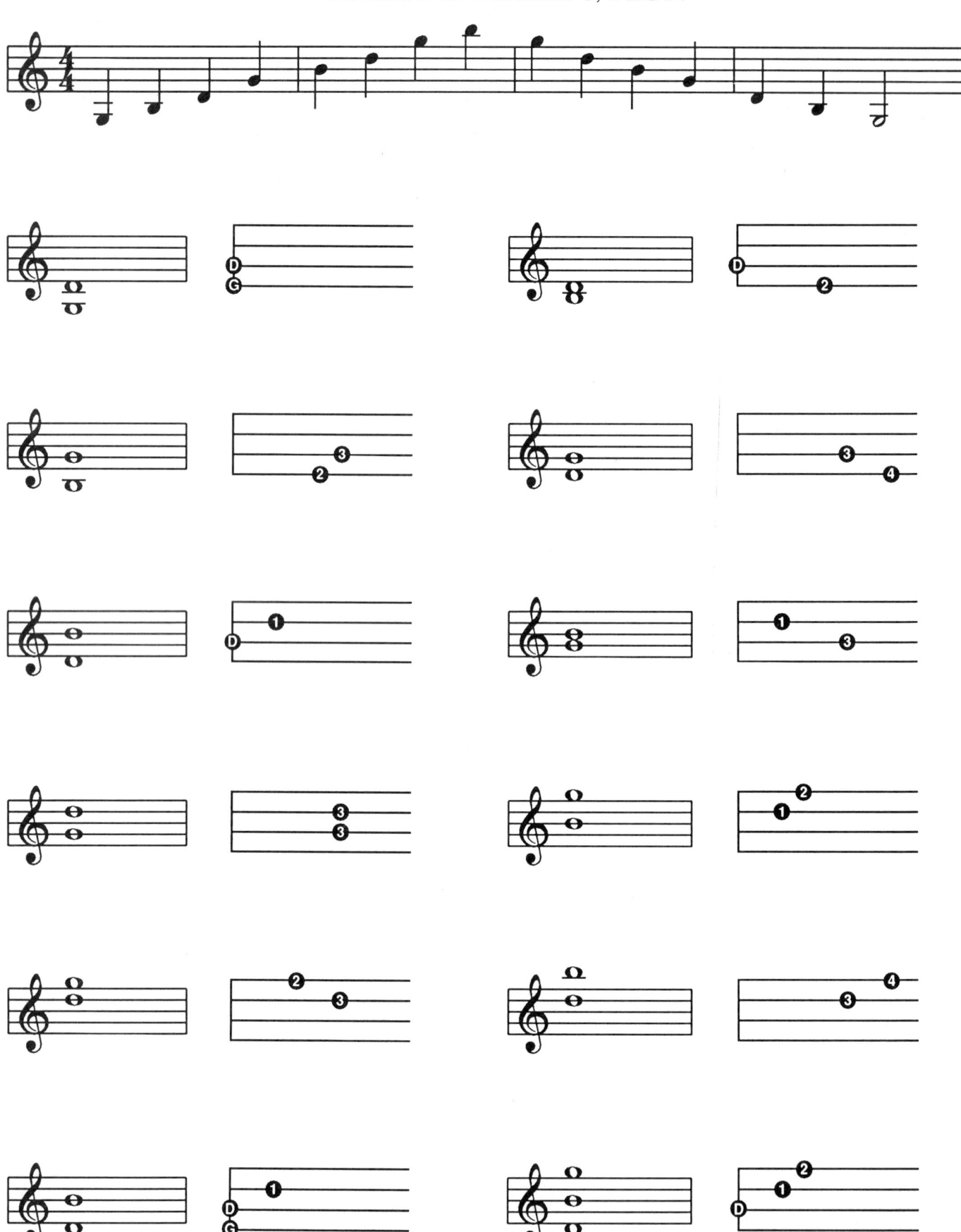

The A♭ Chord

The notes in the A♭ chord are A♭, C and E♭.

The A Chord

The notes in the A chord are A, C♯ and E.

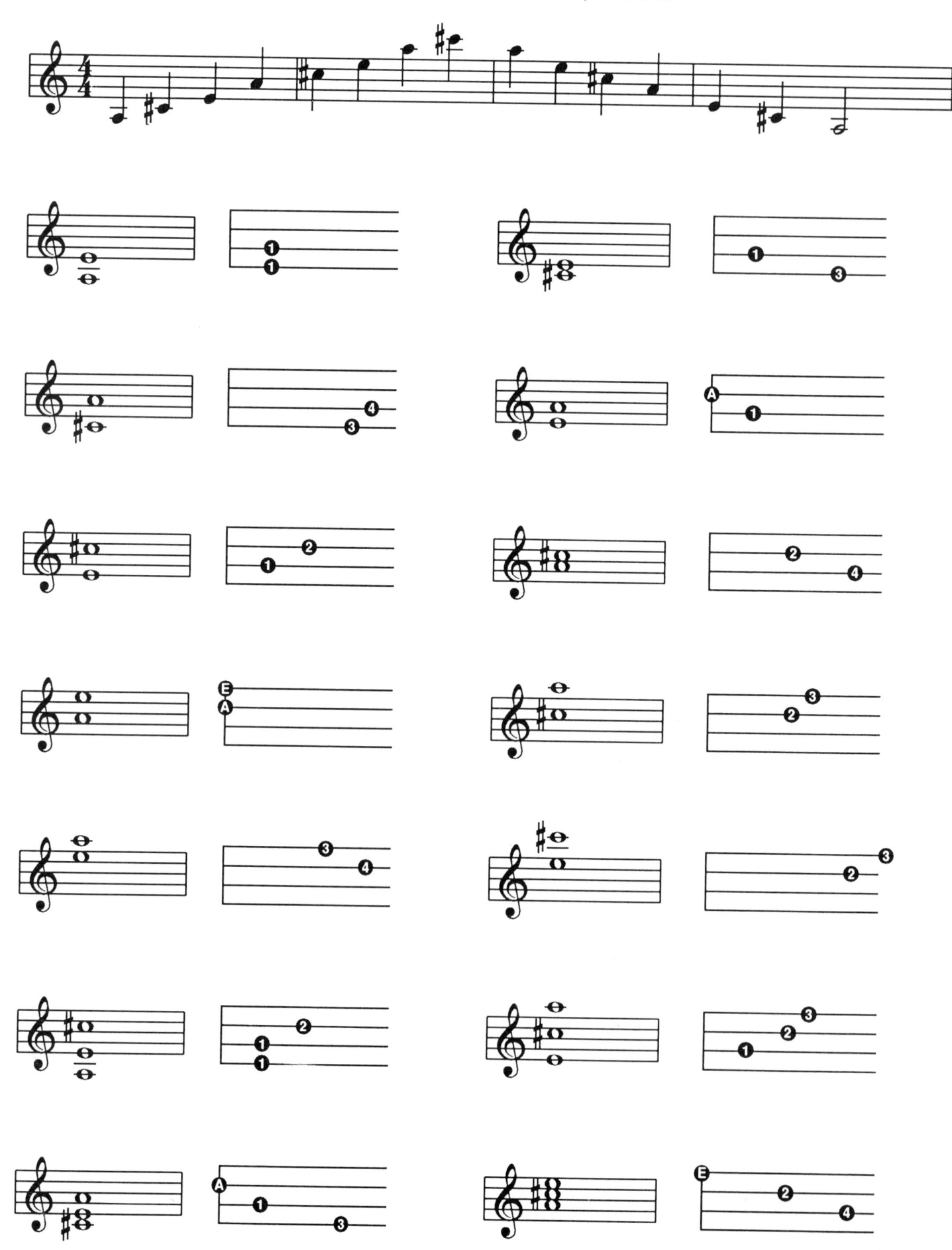

The B♭ Chord

The notes in the B♭ chord are B♭, D and F.

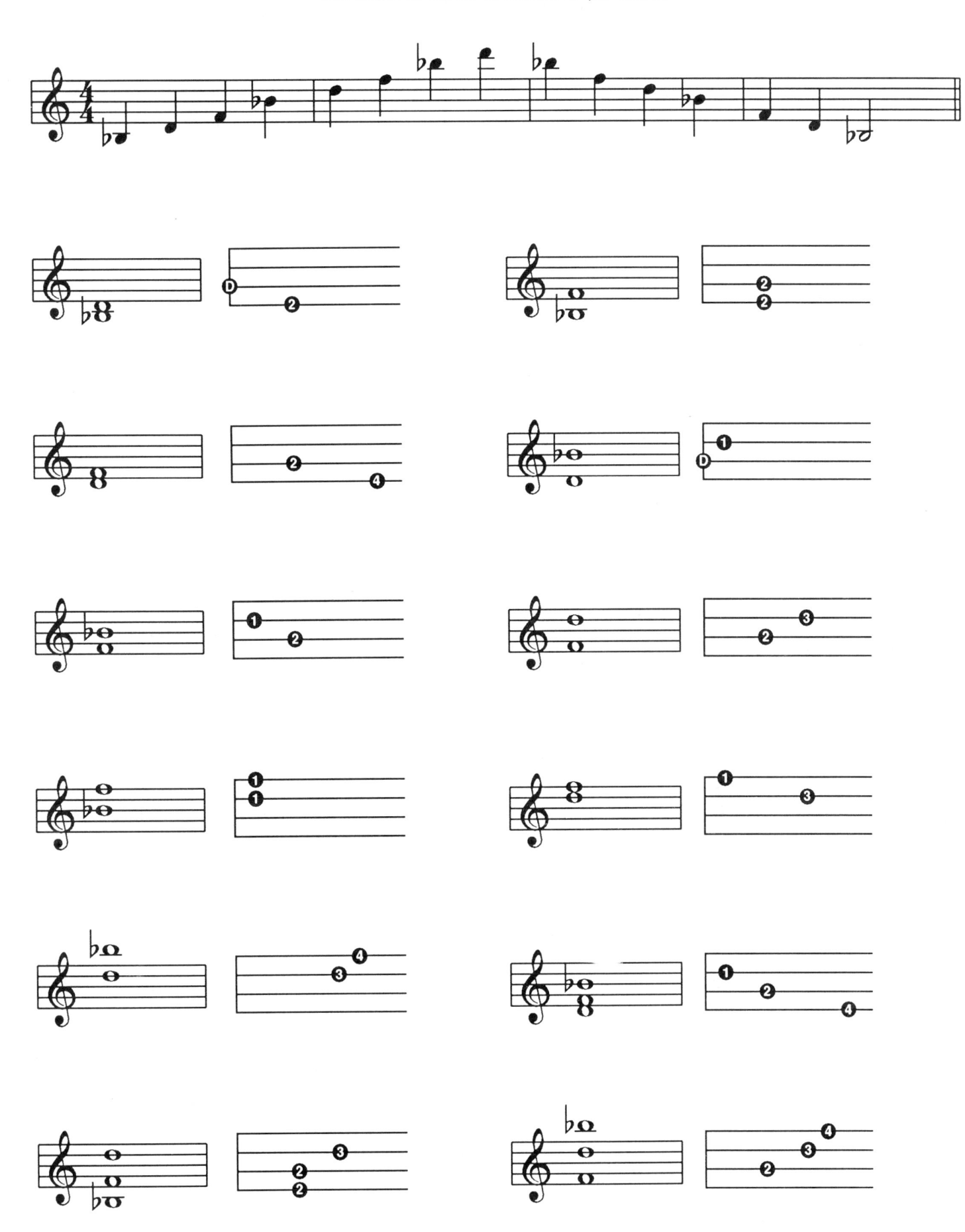

The B Chord

The notes in the B chord are B, D♯ and F♯.

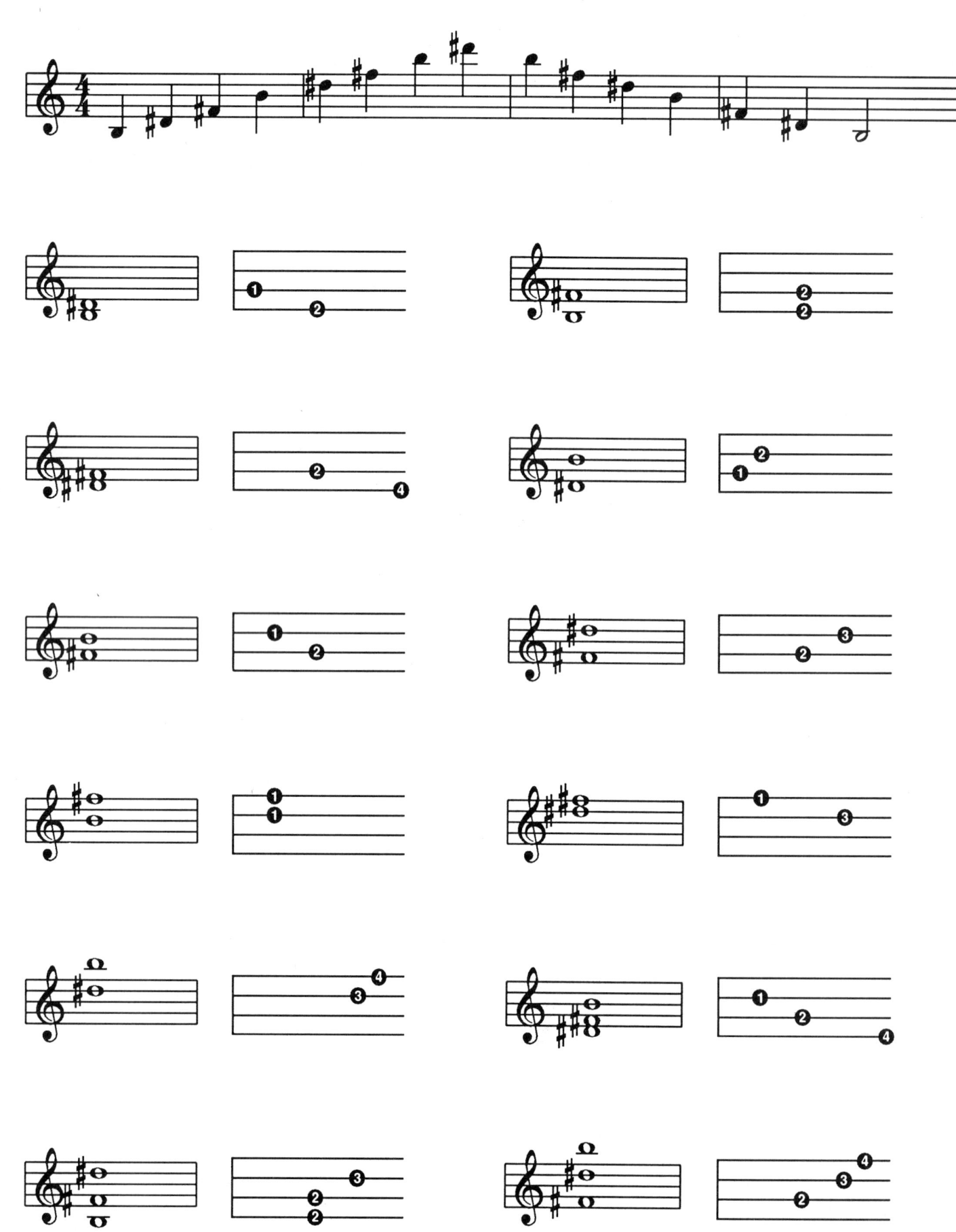

The C Chord

The notes in the C chord are C, E and G.

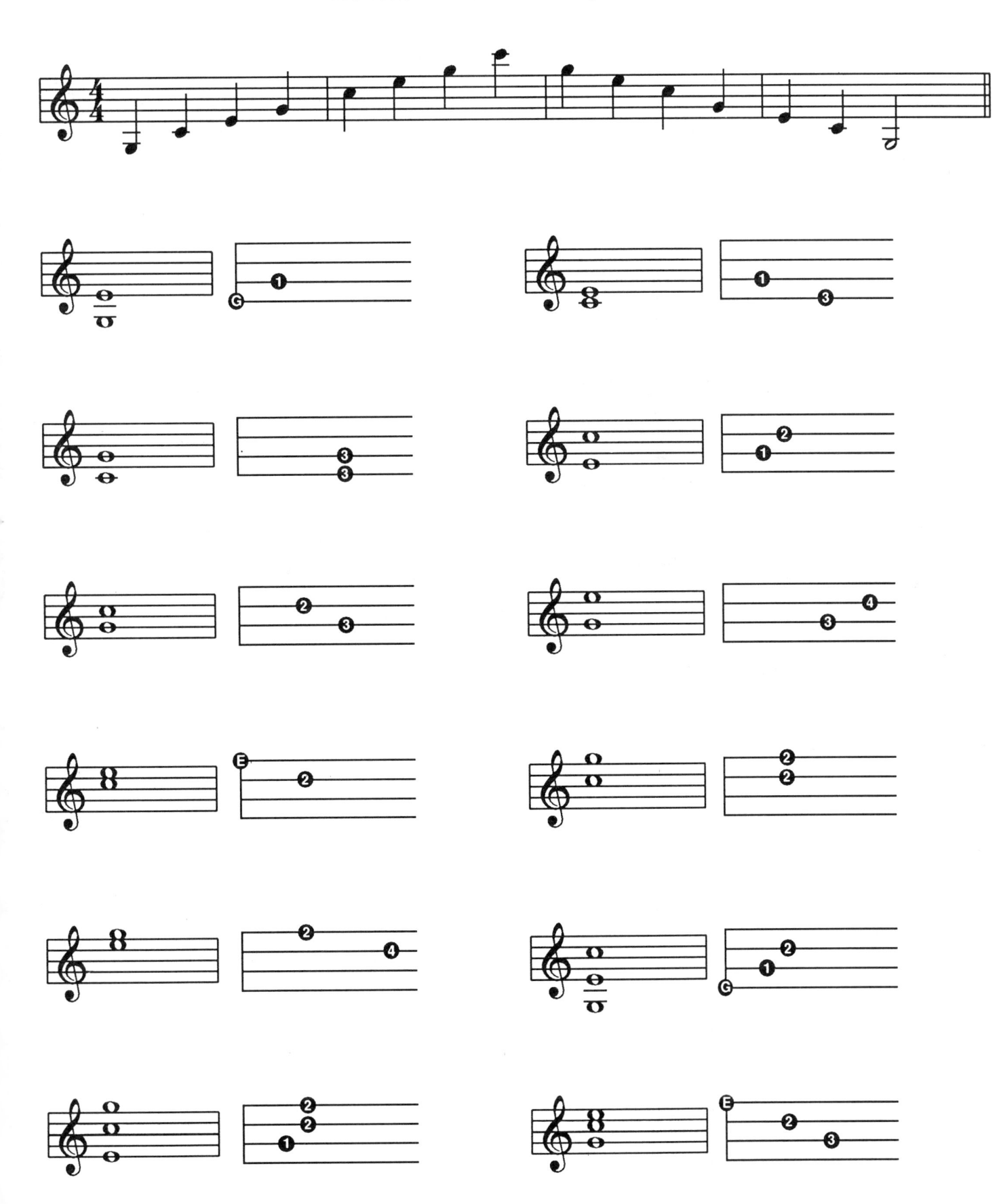

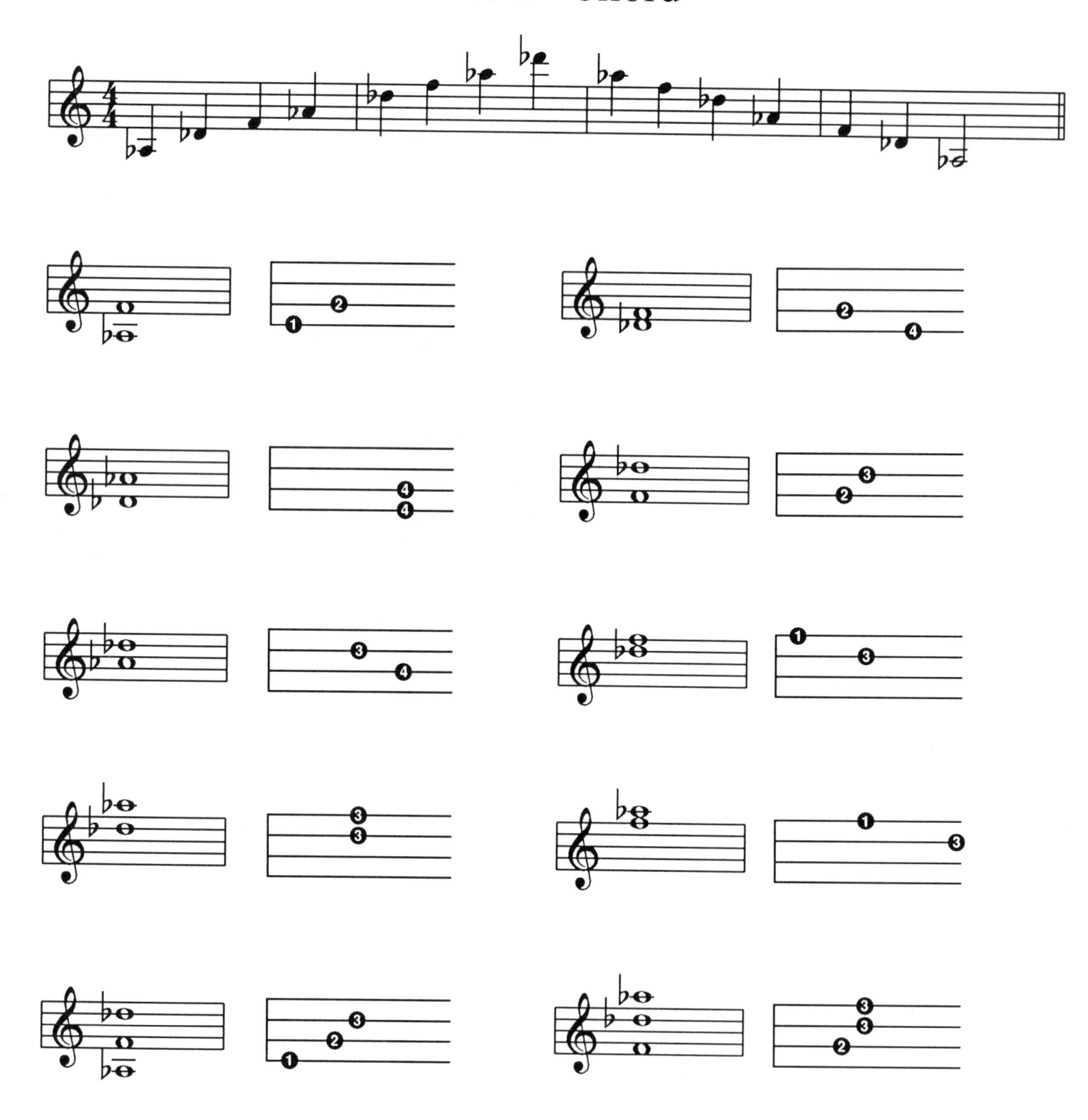

The D♭ Chord

The D Chord

The notes in the D chord are D, F# and A.

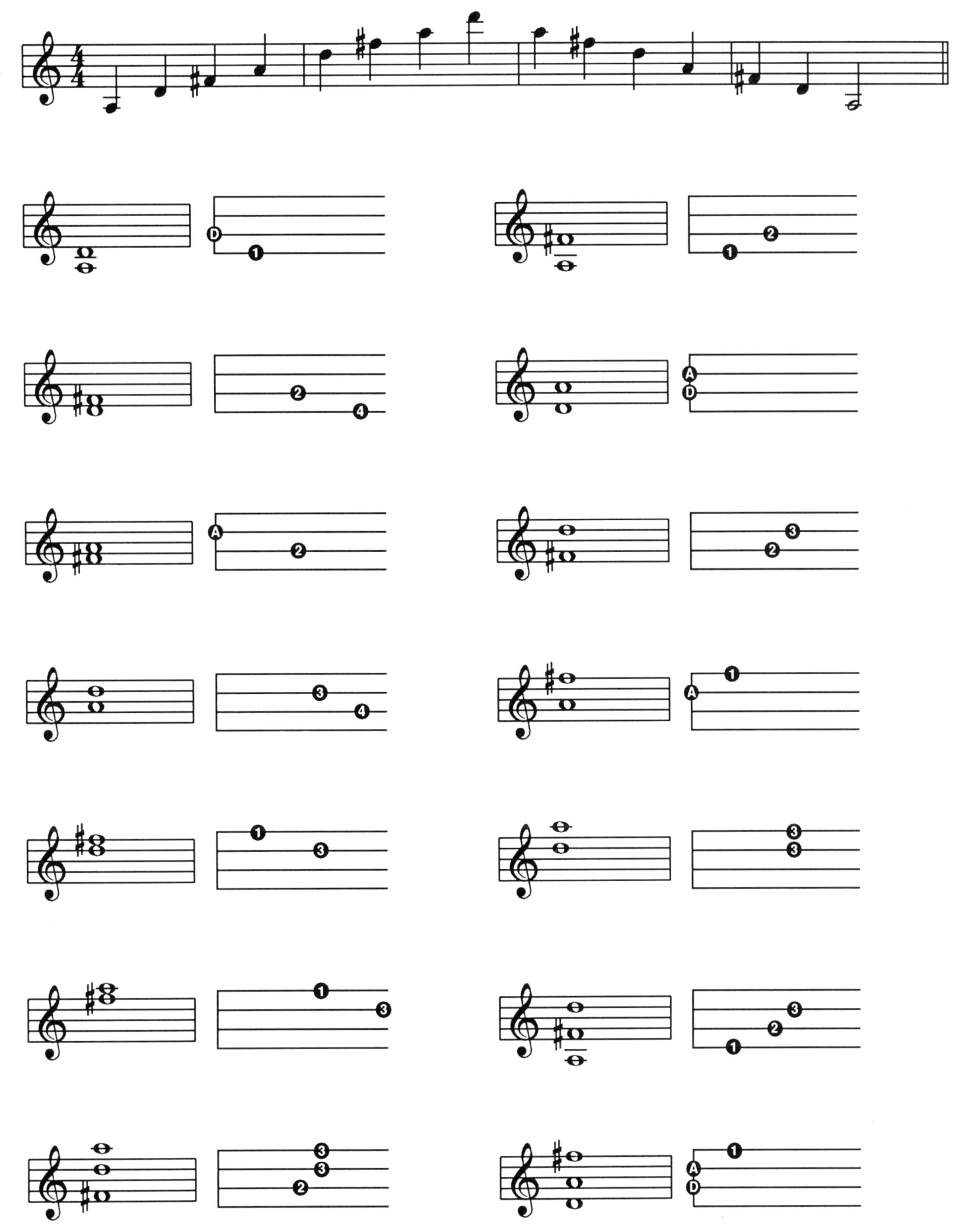

The E♭ Chord

The E Chord

The notes in the E chord are E, G# and B.

The F Chord

The notes in the F chord are F, A and C.

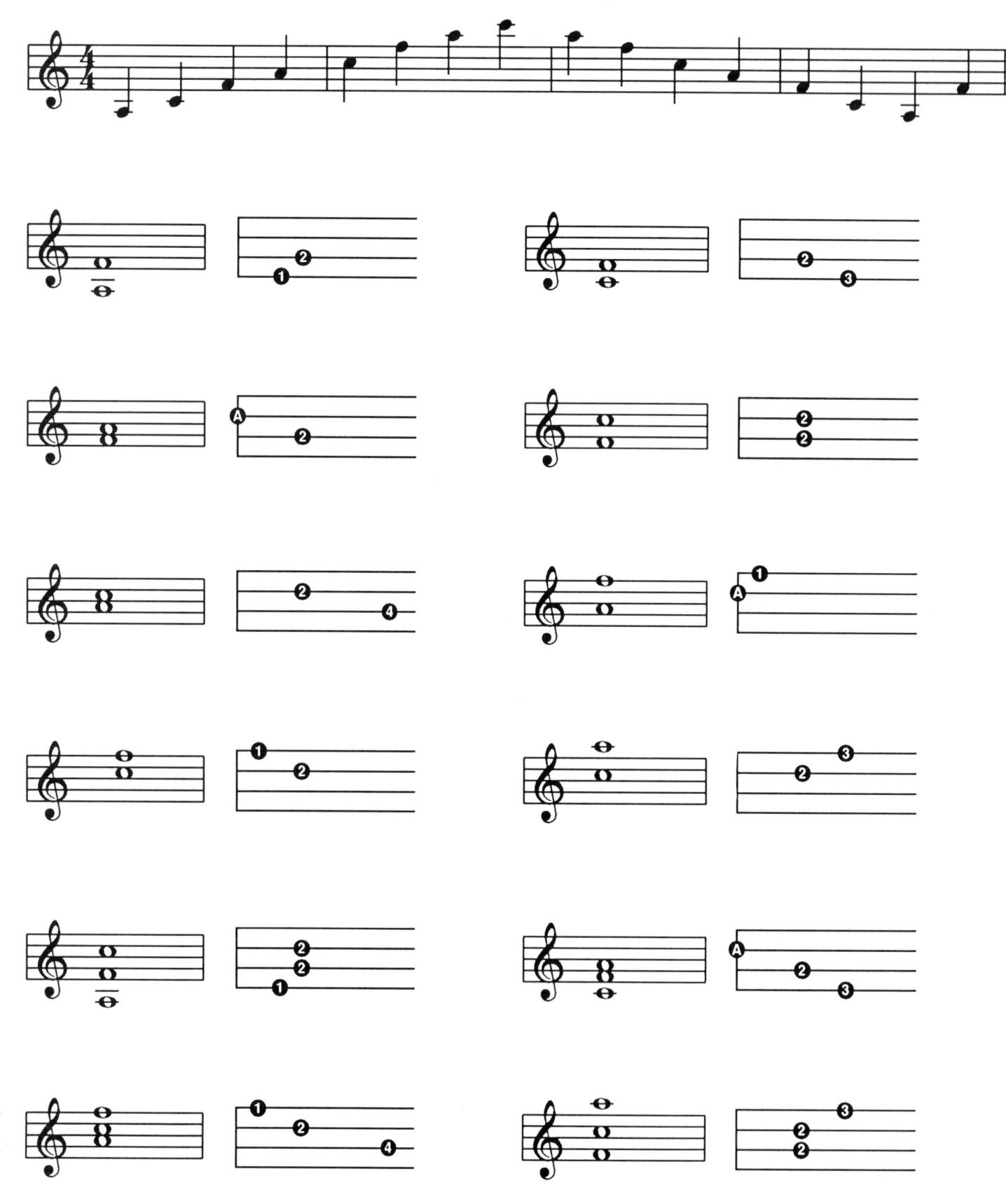

The F# Chord

The notes in the F# chord are F#, A# and C#.

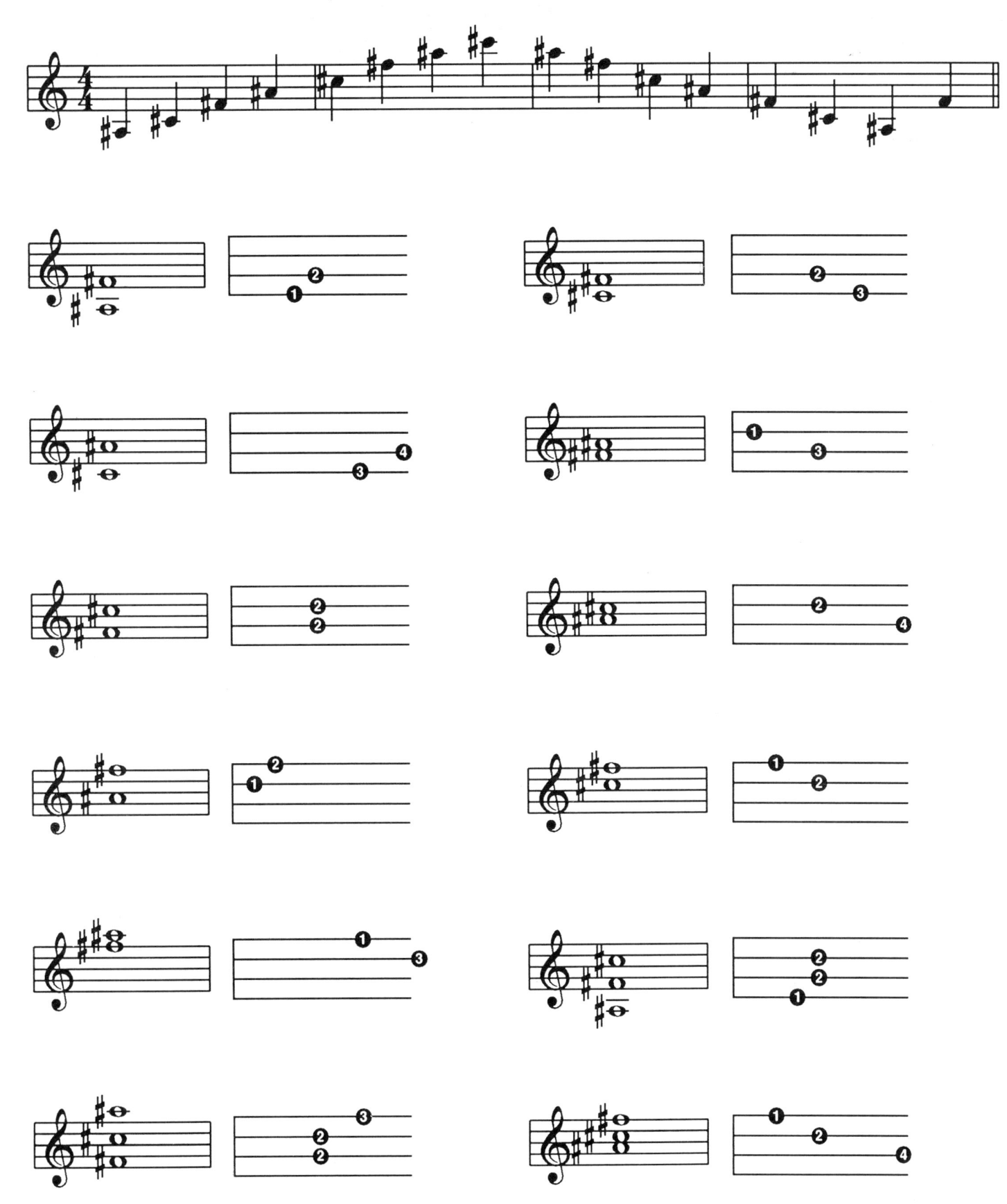

The G Minor Chord

The notes in the G minor chord are G, B♭ and D.

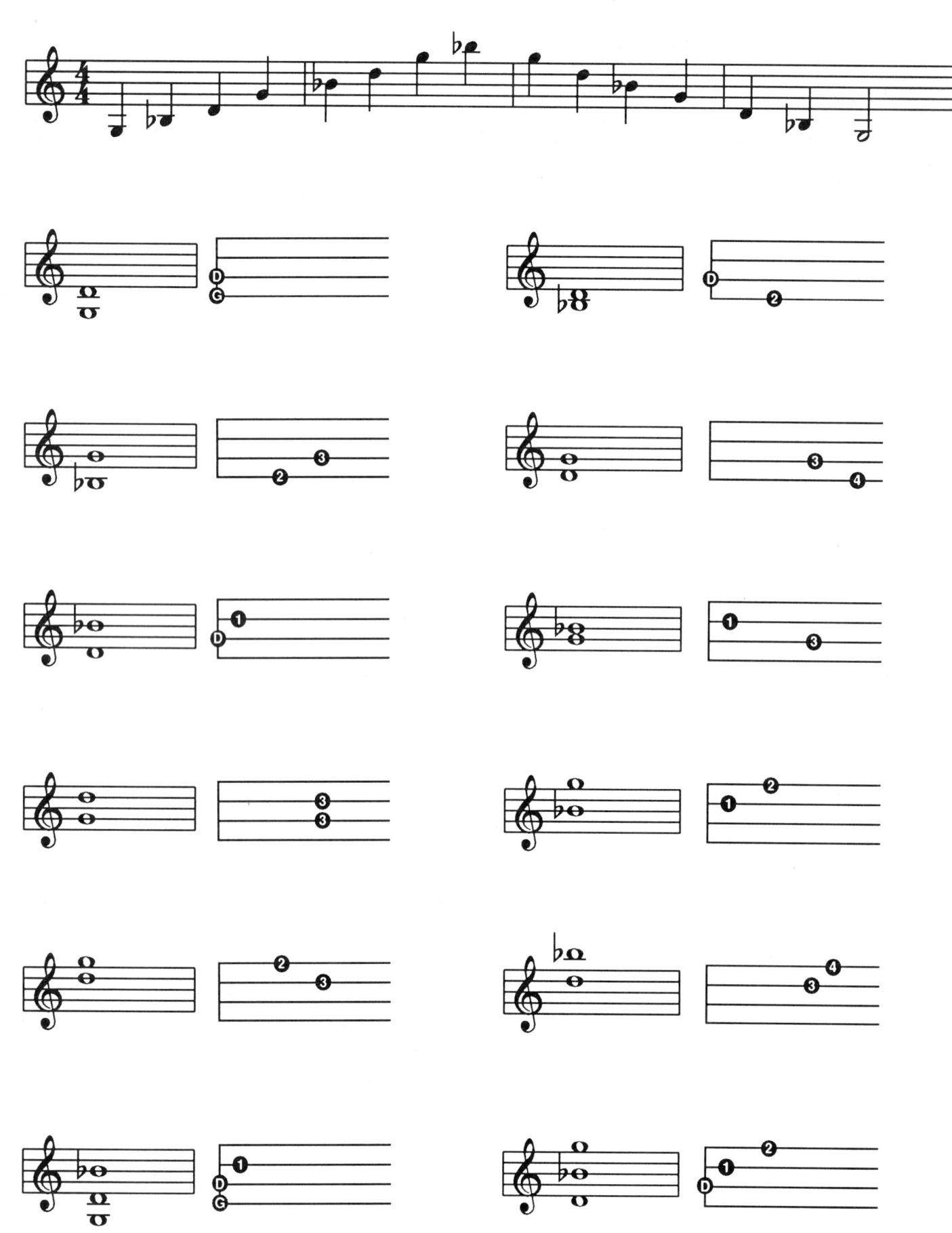

The G# Minor Chord

The notes in the G# minor chord are G#, B and D#.

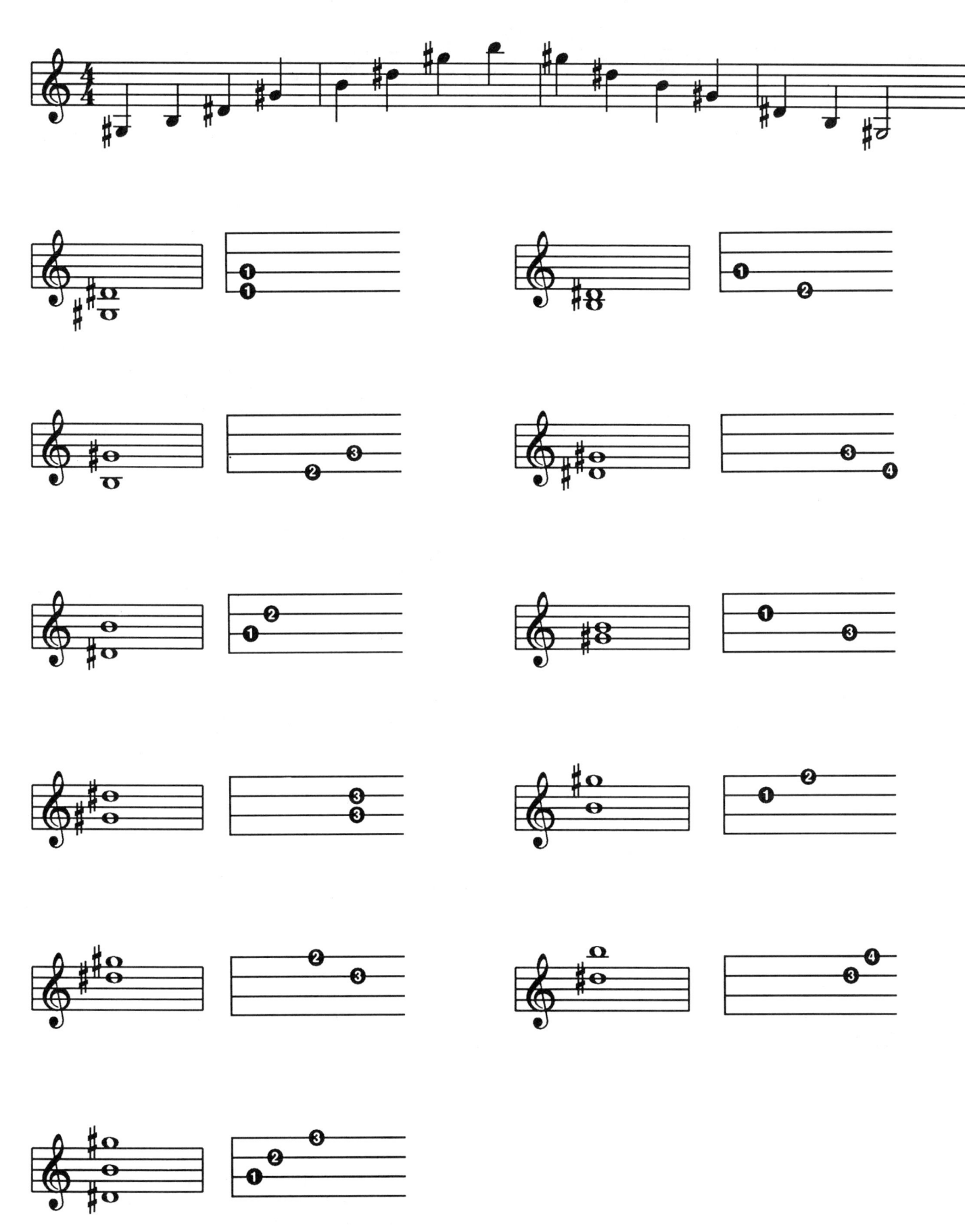

The A Minor Chord

The notes in the A minor chord are A, C and E.

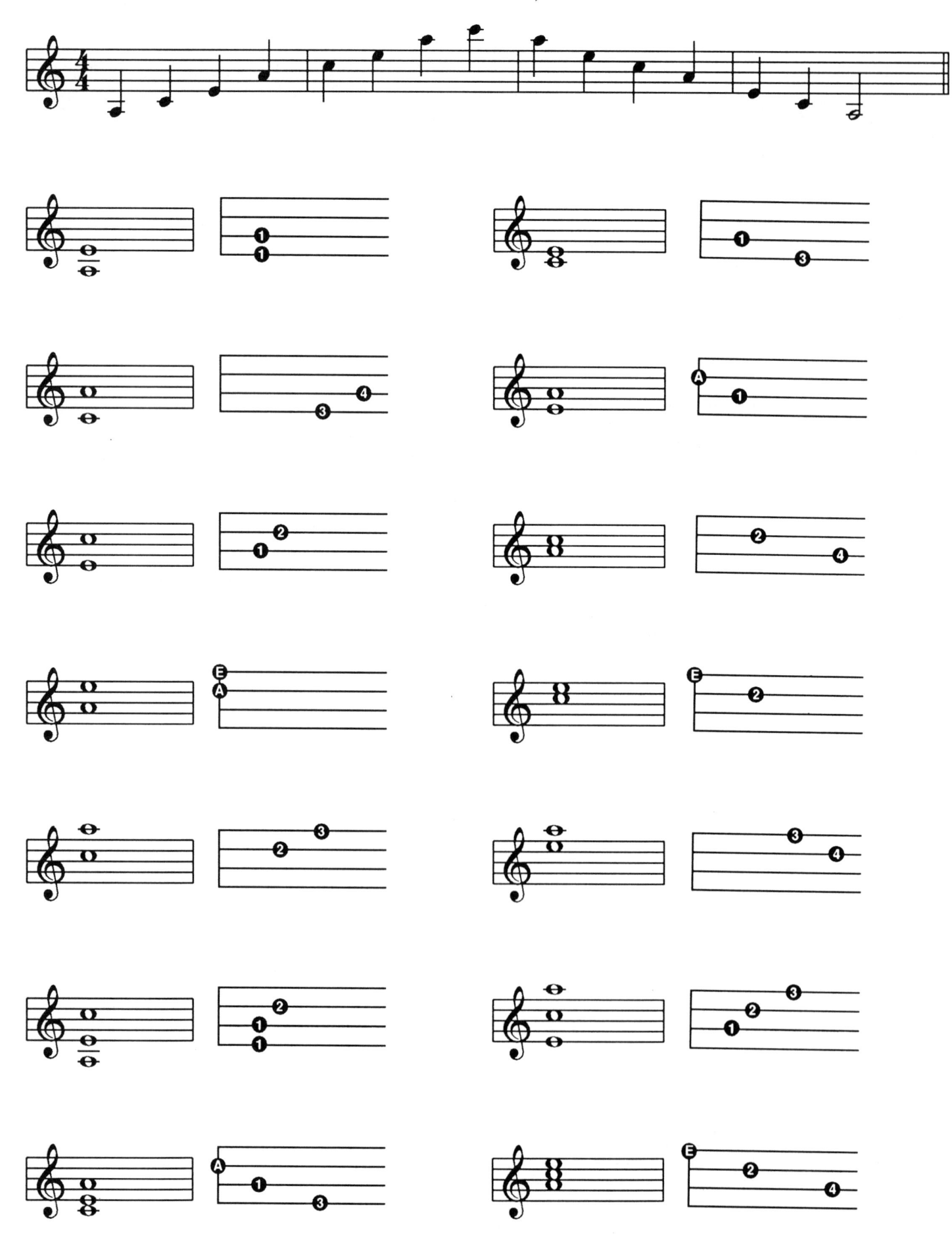

The B♭ Minor Chord

The notes in the B♭ minor chord are B♭, D♭ and F.

The B Minor Chord

The notes in the B minor chord are B, D and F#.

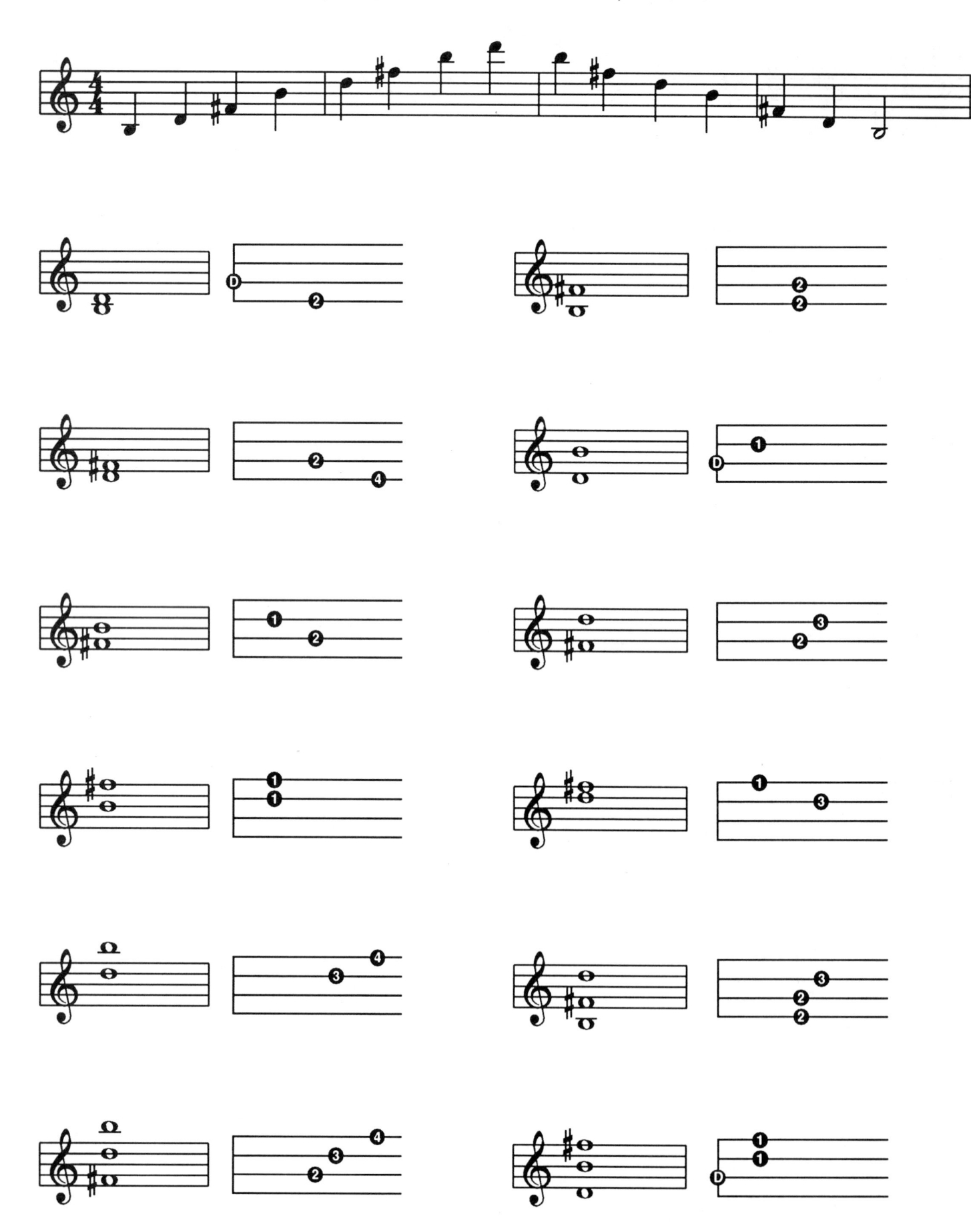

The C Minor Chord

The notes in the C minor chord are C, E♭ and G.

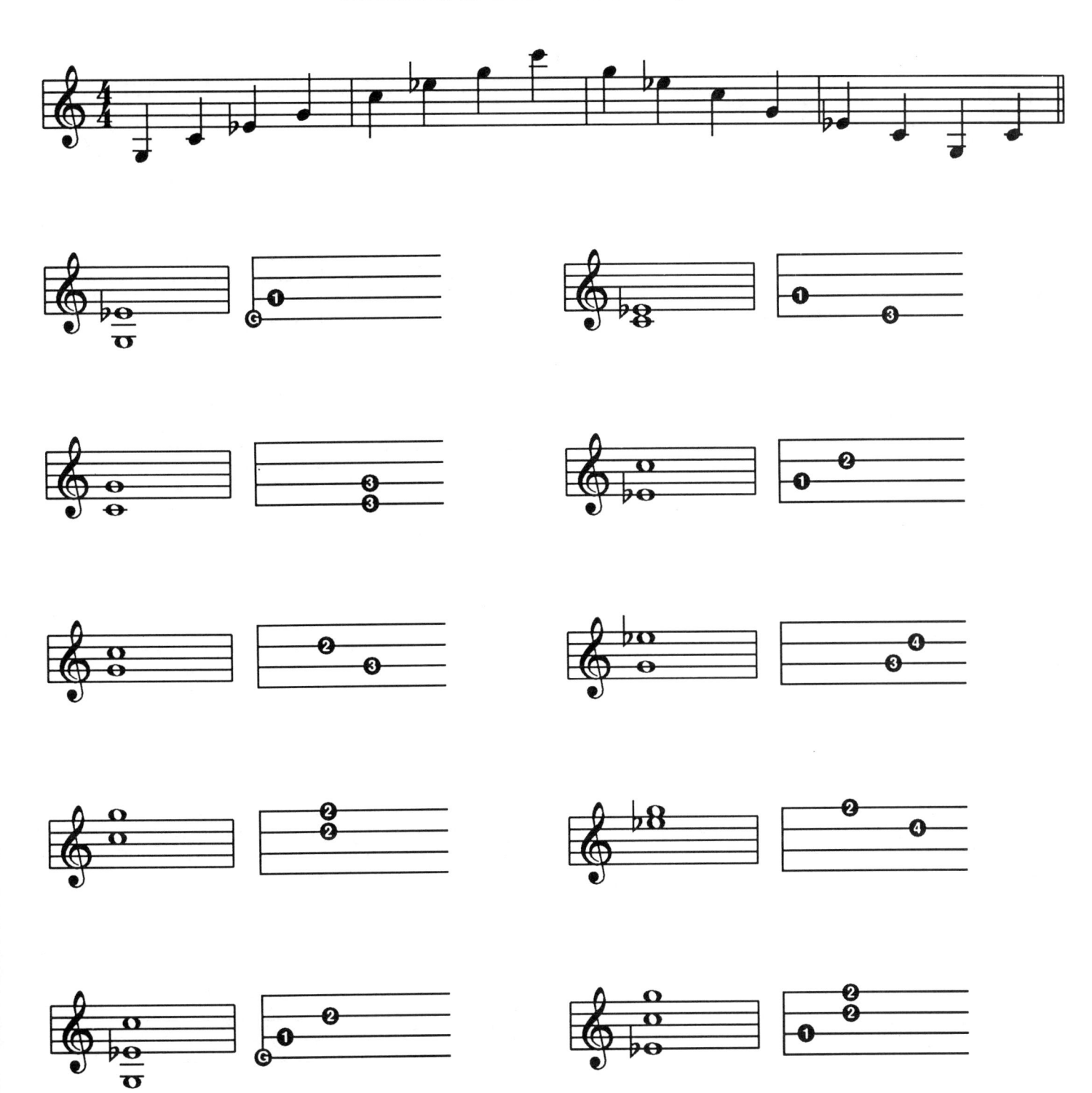

The C# Minor Chord

The notes in the C# minor chord are C#, E and G#.

The D Minor Chord

The notes in the D minor chord are D, F and A.

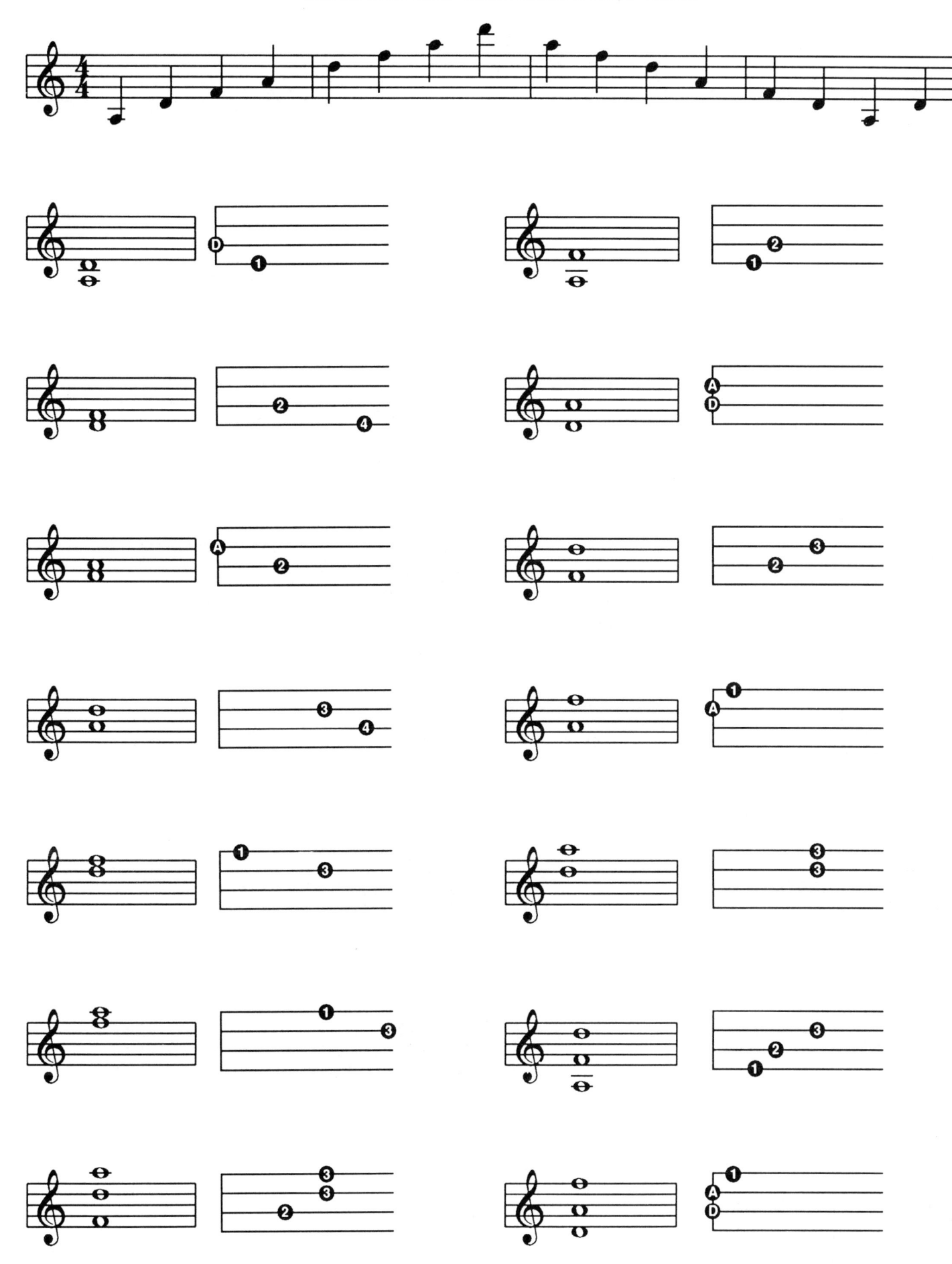

The D♯ Minor Chord

The notes in the D♯ minor chord are D♯, F♯ and A♯.

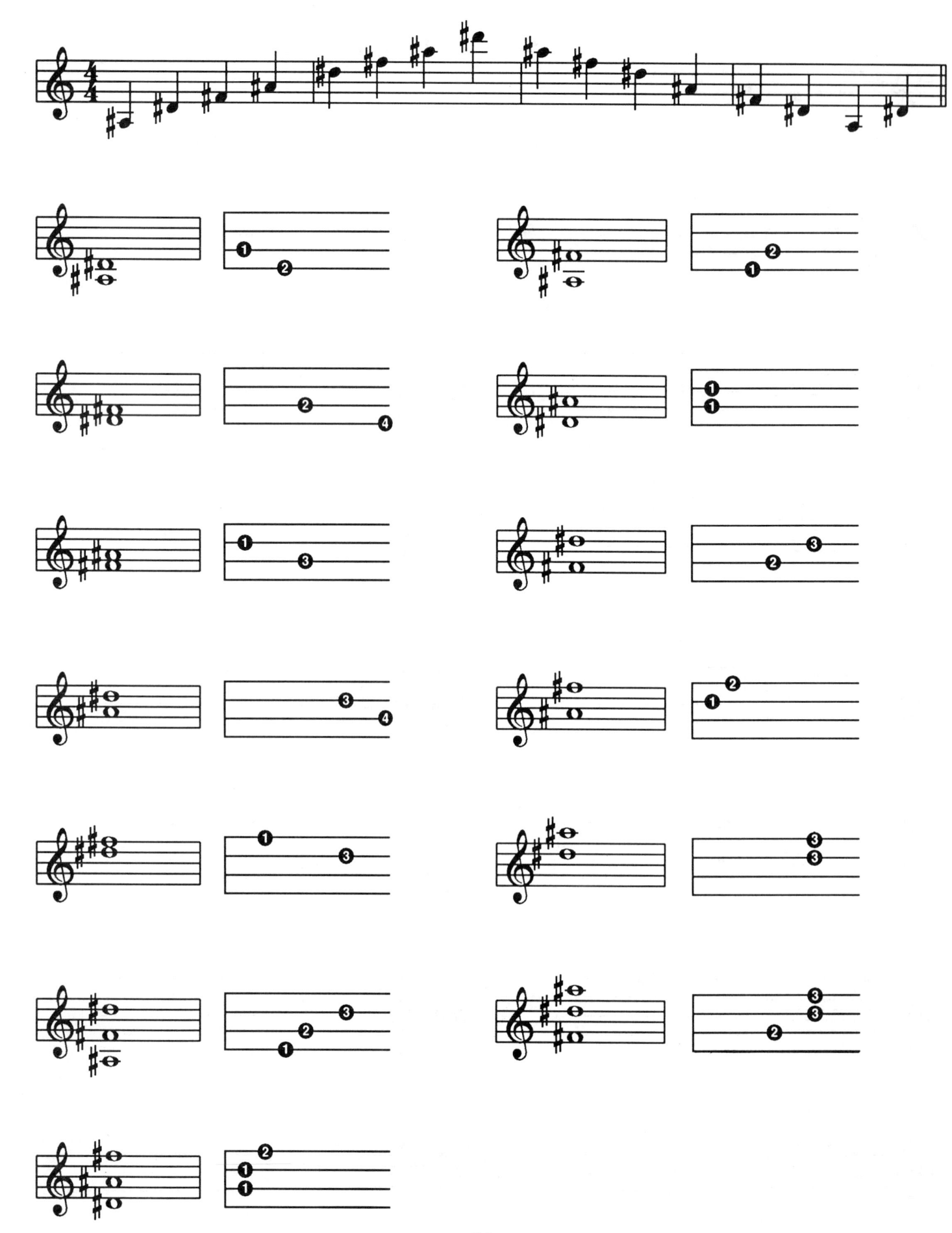

The E Minor Chord

The notes in the E minor chord are E, G and B.

The F Minor Chord
The notes in the F minor chord are F, A♭ and C.

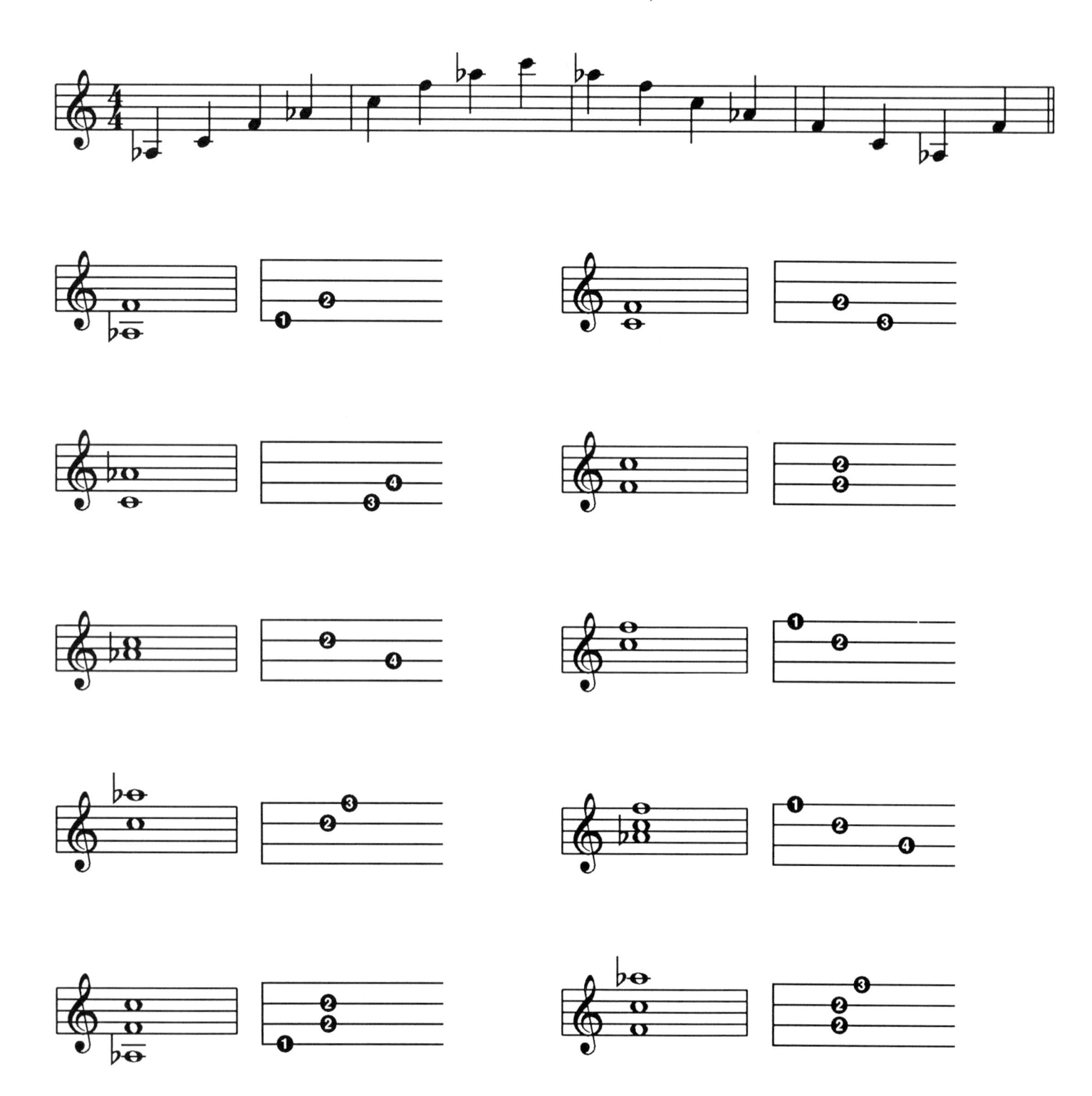

The F# Minor Chord

The notes in the F# minor chord are F#, A and C#.

The G, (A♯) B♭, (C♯) D♭, E Diminished Chord

These notes are all in the same diminished chord. The name of the chord
is determined by what note is played in the bass as the lowest note.

28

The G#, B, D, F Diminished Chord

These notes are all in the same diminished chord. The name of the chord is determined by what note is played in the bass as the lowest note.

The A, C, (D♯) E♭, F♯ (G♭) Diminished Chord

These notes are all in the same diminished chord. The name of the chord
is determined by what note is played in the bass as the lowest note.

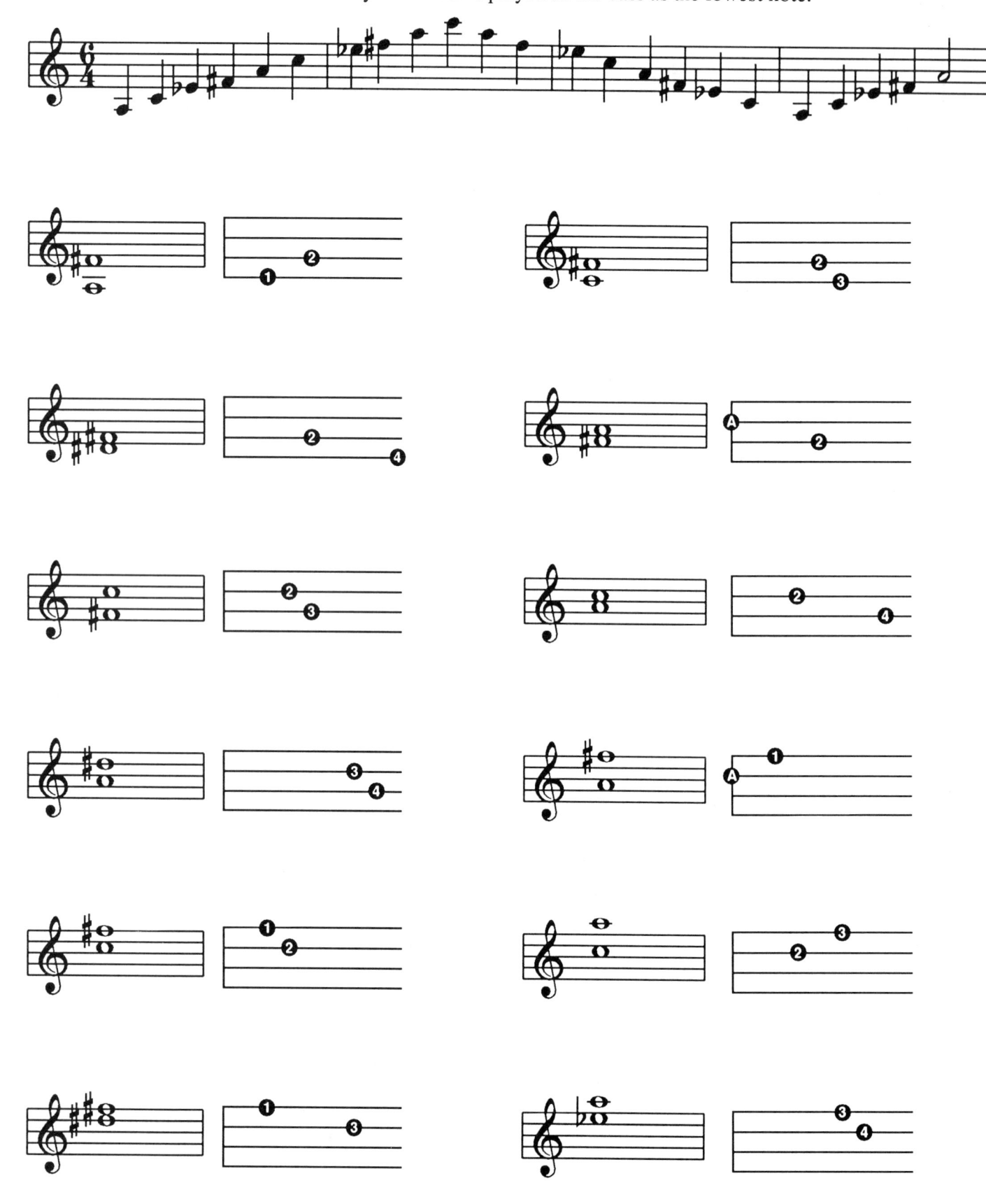

The G, B, (D♯) E♭ Augmented Chord

These notes are all in the same augmented chord. The name of the chord is determined by what note is played in the bass as the lowest note.

The A♭, C, E Augmented Chord

These notes are all in the same augmented chord. The name of the chord is determined by what note is played in the bass as the lowest note.

The A, C♯ (D♭), (E♯) F Augmented Chord

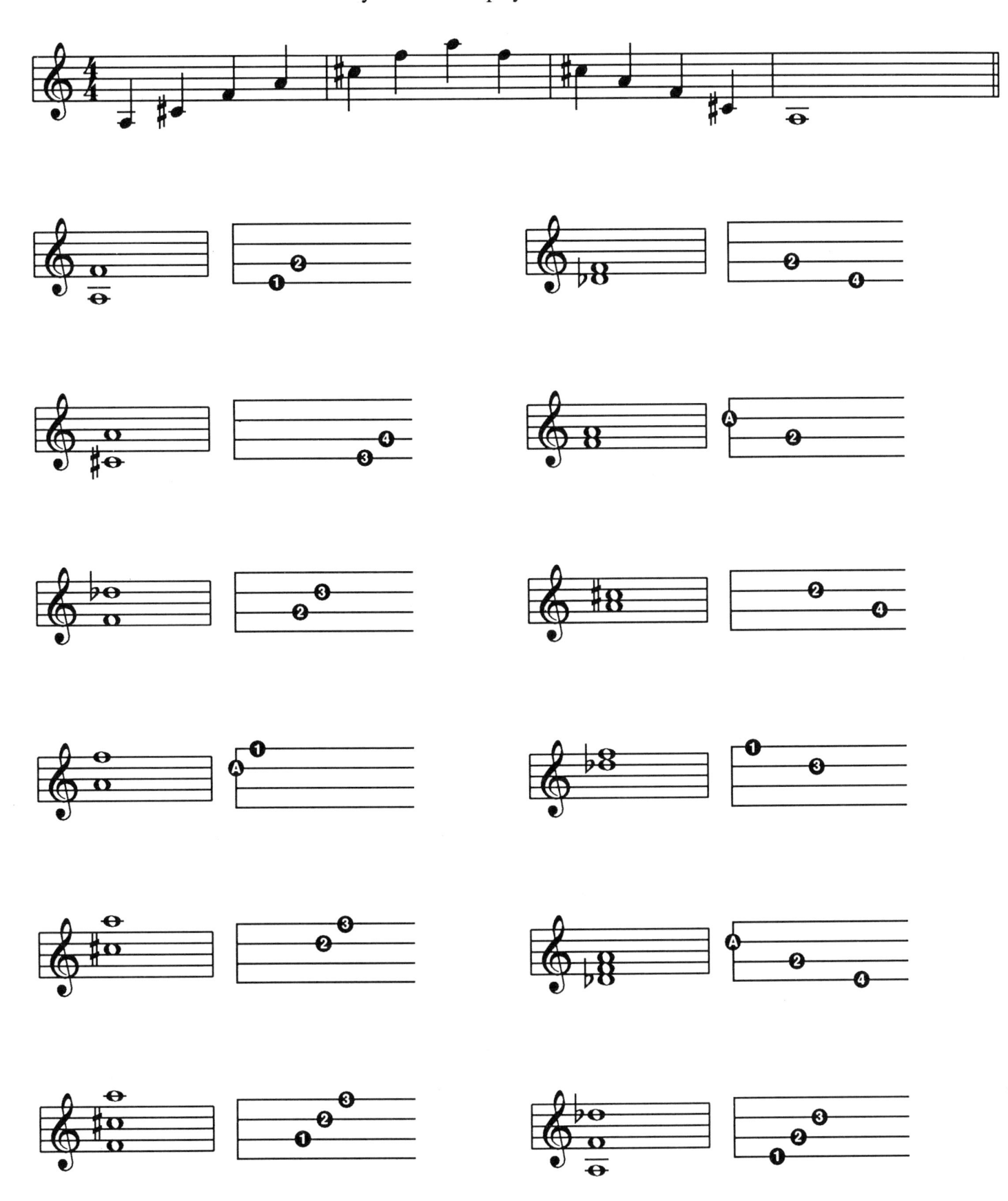

These notes are all in the same augmented chord. The name of the chord
is determined by what note is played in the bass as the lowest note.

The (A♯) B♭, D, (F♯) G♭ Augmented Chord

These notes are all in the same augmented chord. The name of the chord
is determined by what note is played in the bass as the lowest note.

The G7 Chord

The notes in the G7 chord are G, B, D and F.

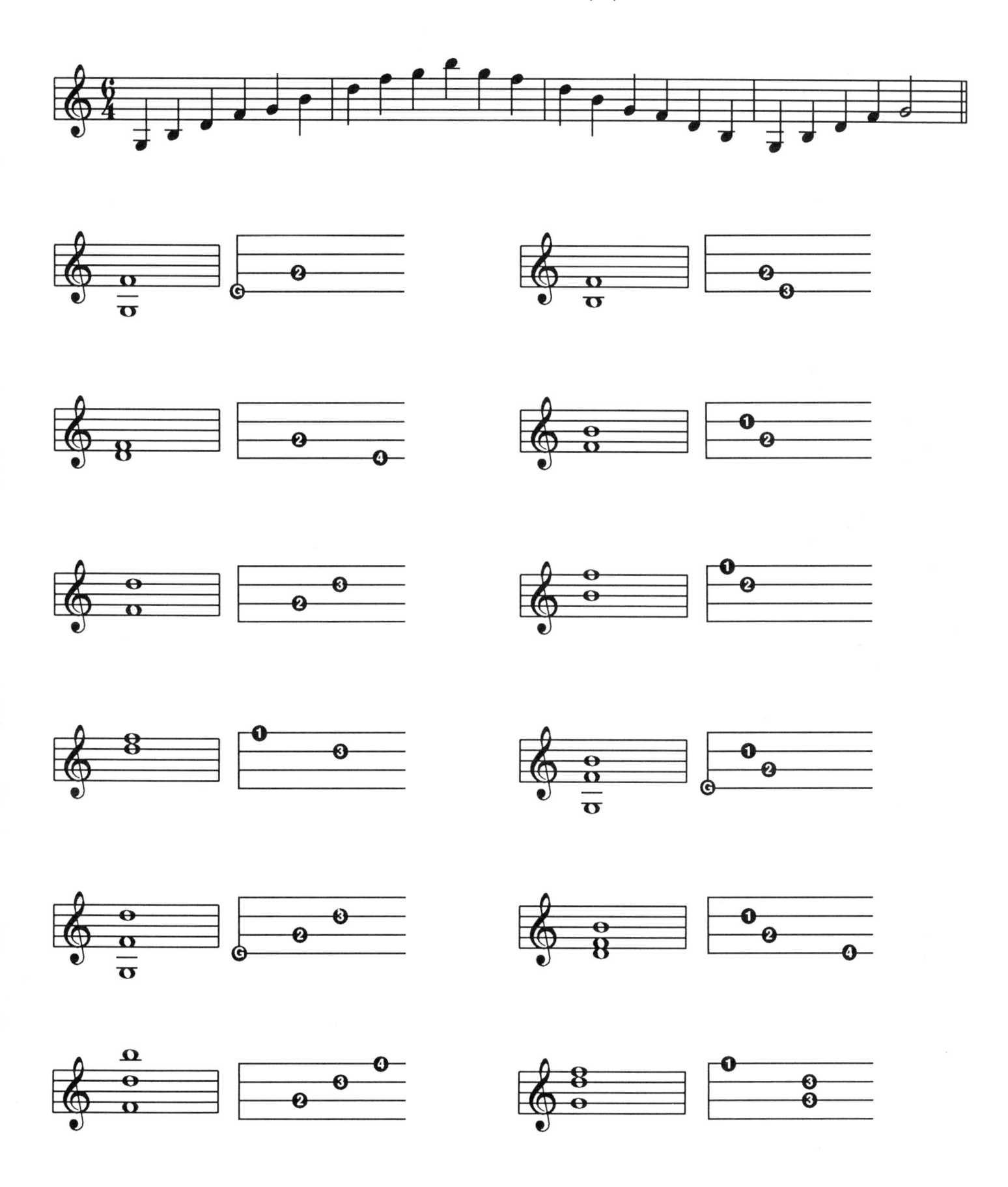

The A♭7 Chord

The notes in the A♭7 chord are A♭, C, E♭ and G♭.

The A7 Chord

The notes in the A7 chord are A, C#, E and G.

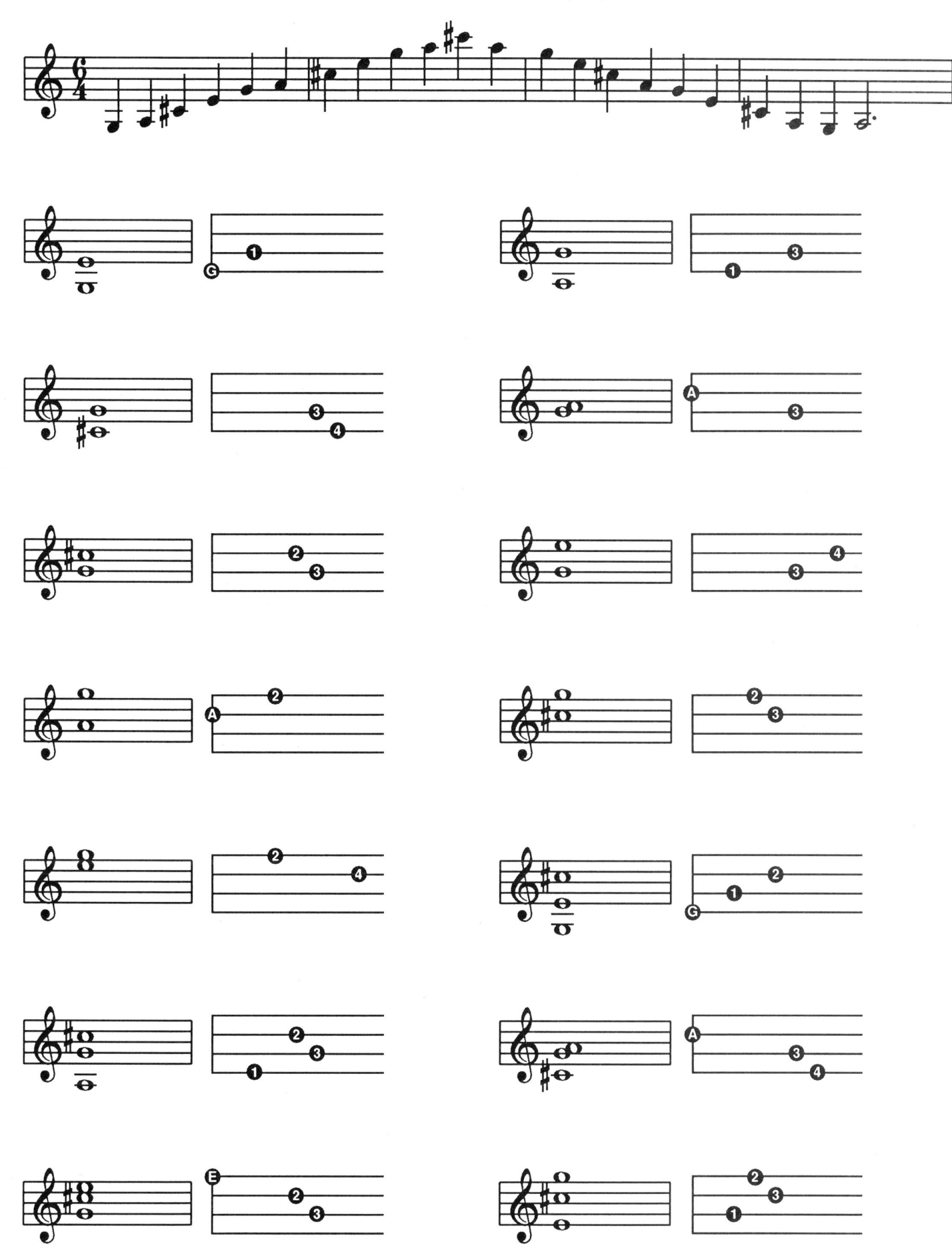

The B♭7 Chord

The notes in the B♭7 chord are B♭, D, F and A♭.

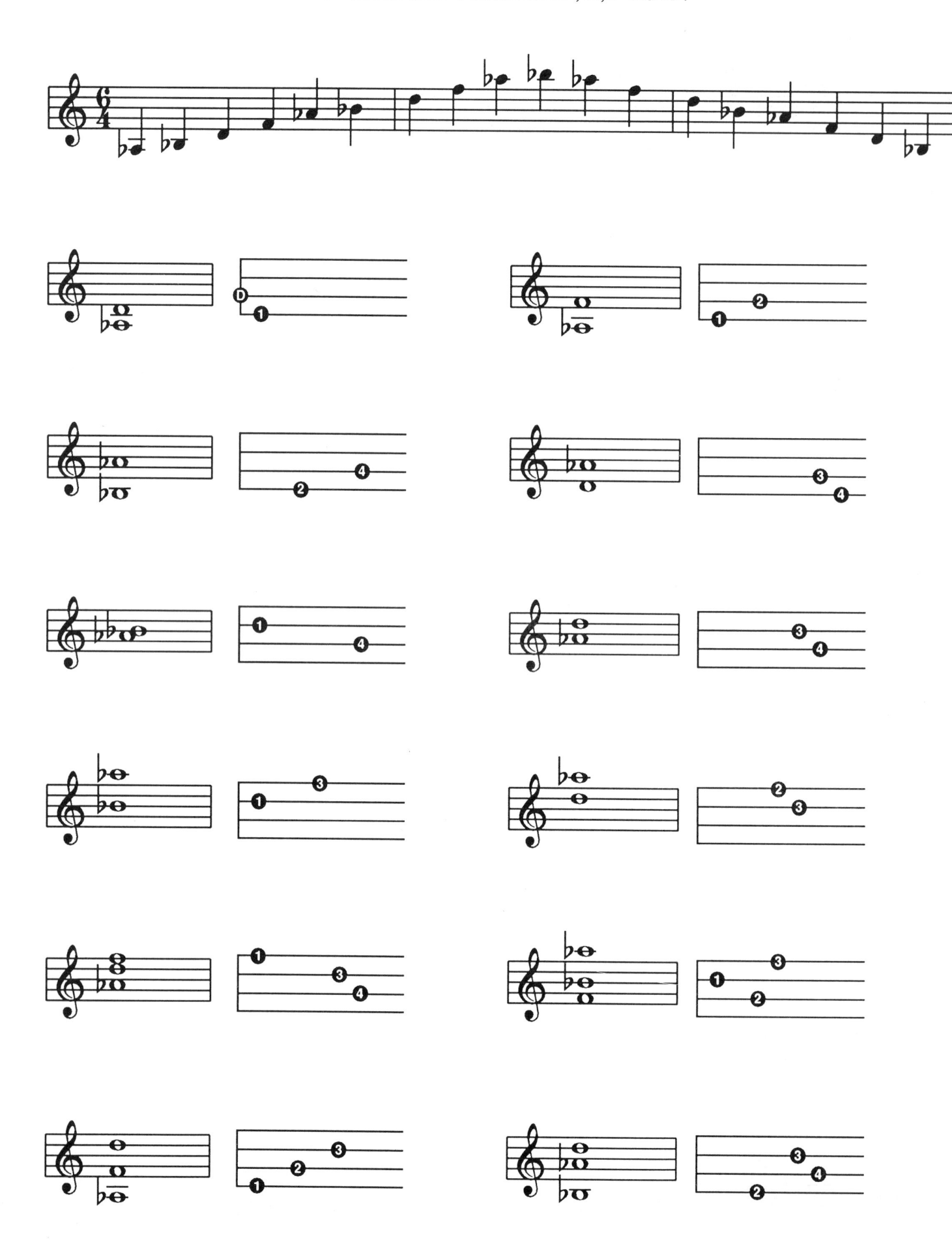

The B7 Chord

The notes in the B7 chord are B, D#, F# and A.

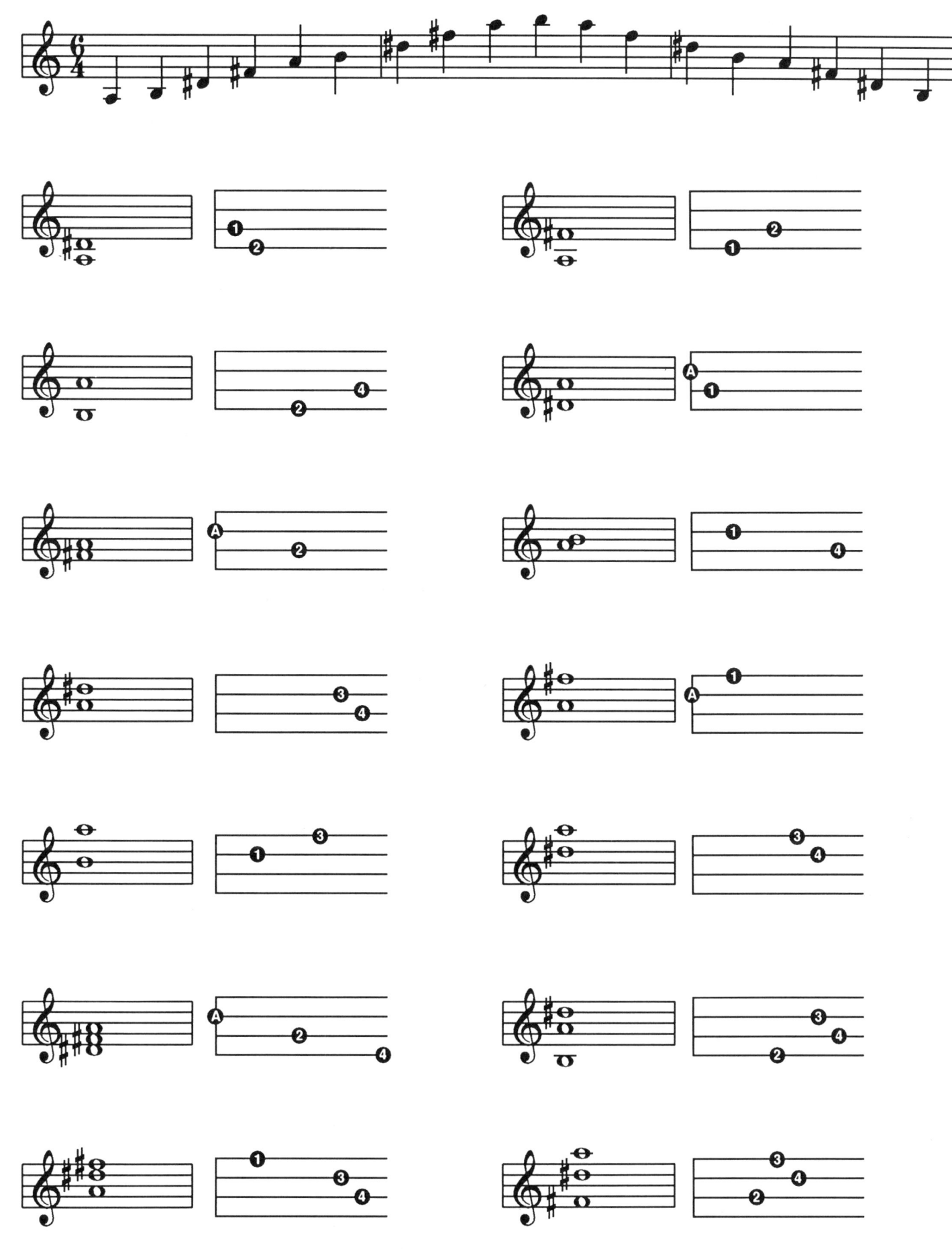

The C7 Chord

The notes in the C7 chord are C, E, G and B♭.

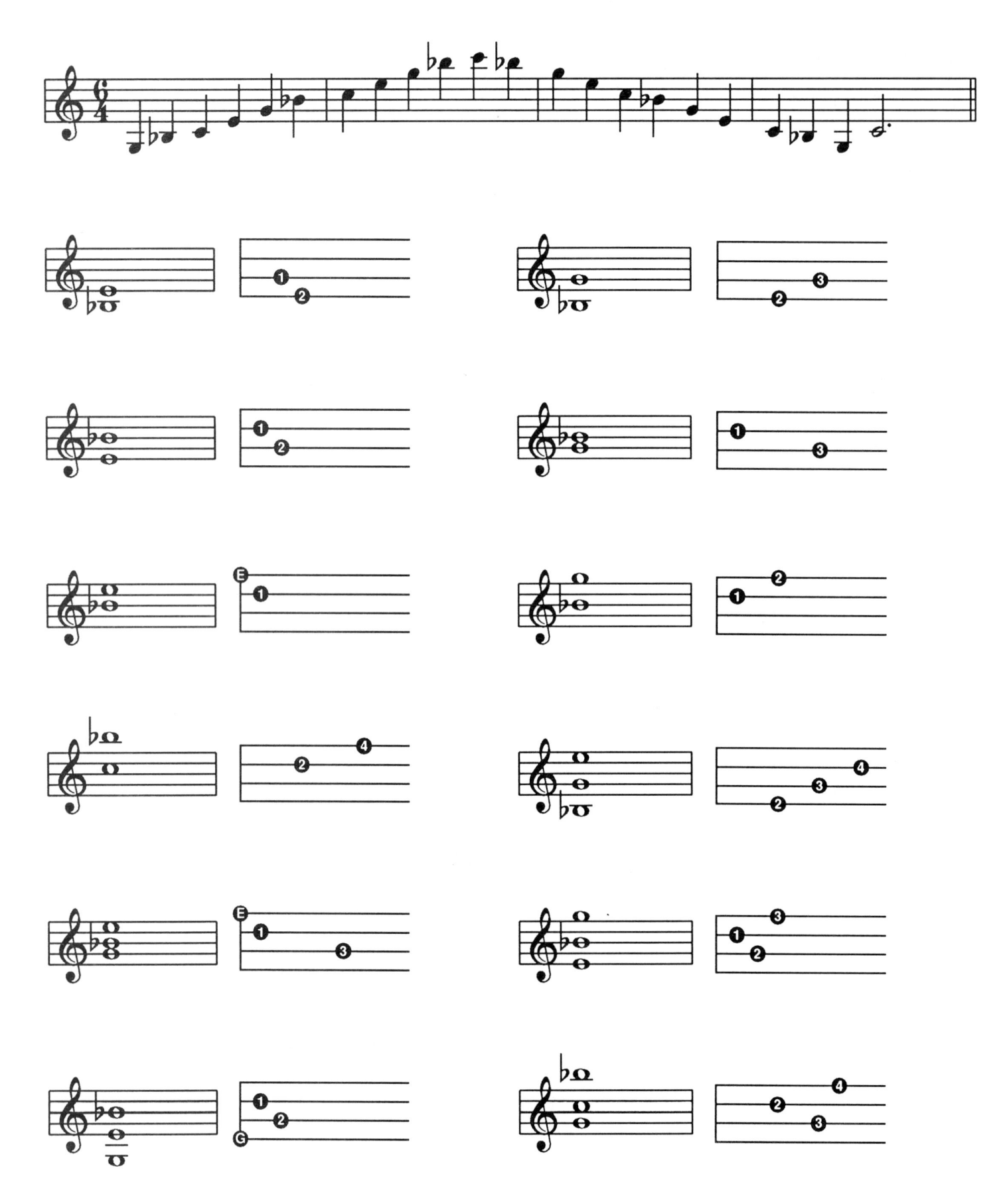

The C#7 Chord

The notes in the C#7 chord are C#, E#, G# and B.

The D7 Chord
The notes in the D7 chord are D, F#, A and C.

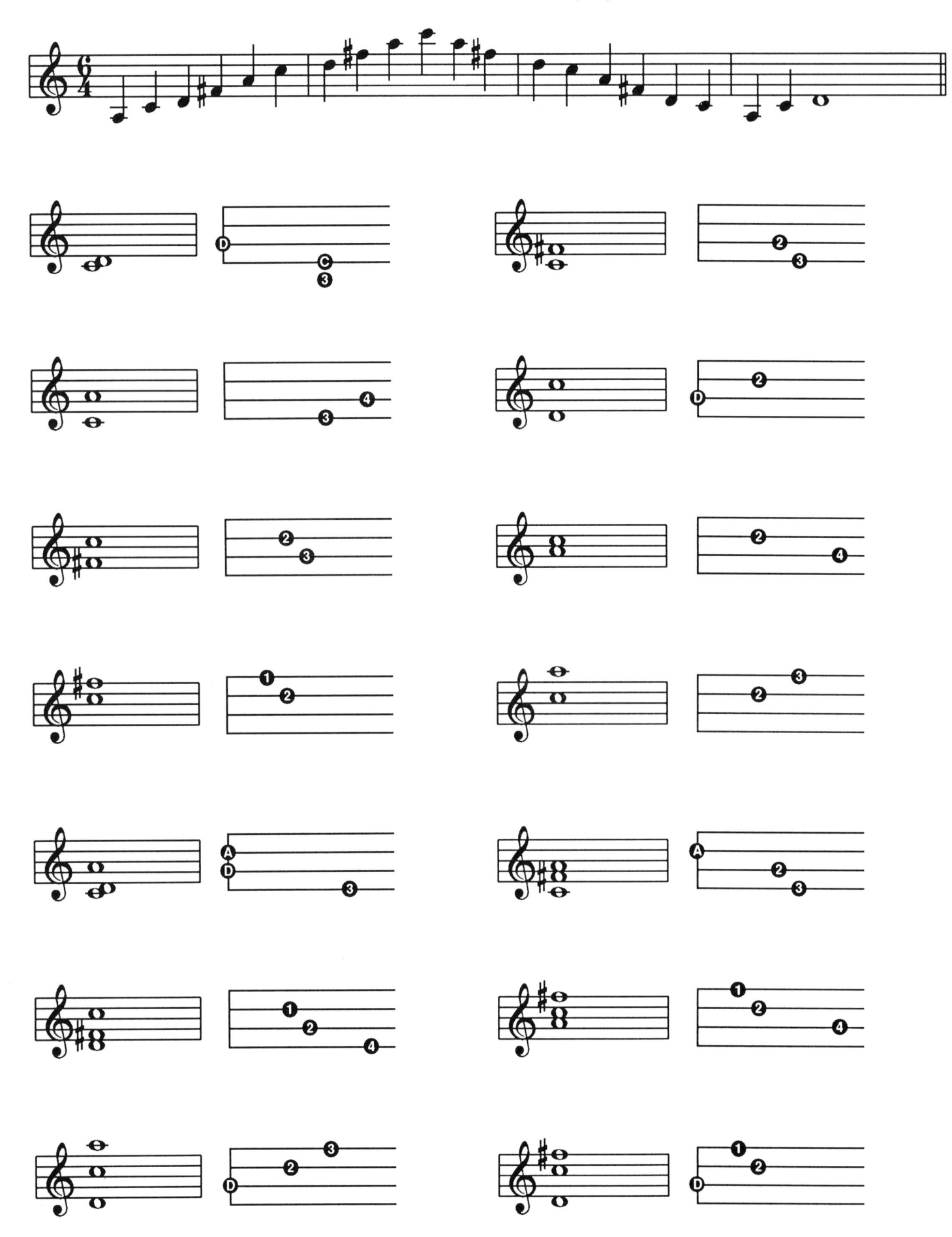

The E♭7 Chord

The notes in the E♭7 chord are E♭, G, B♭ and D♭.

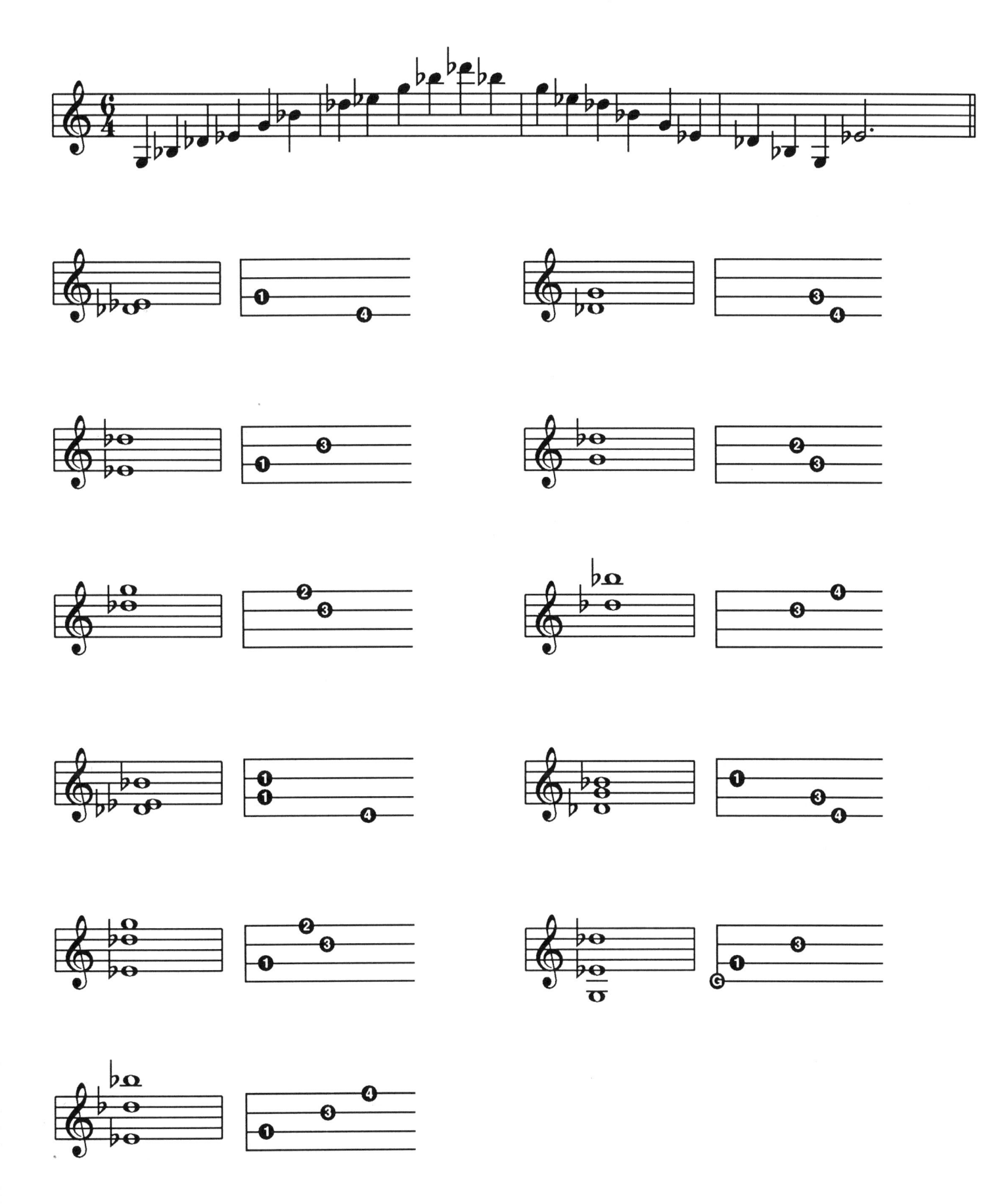

The E7 Chord

The notes in the E7 chord are E, G#, B and D.

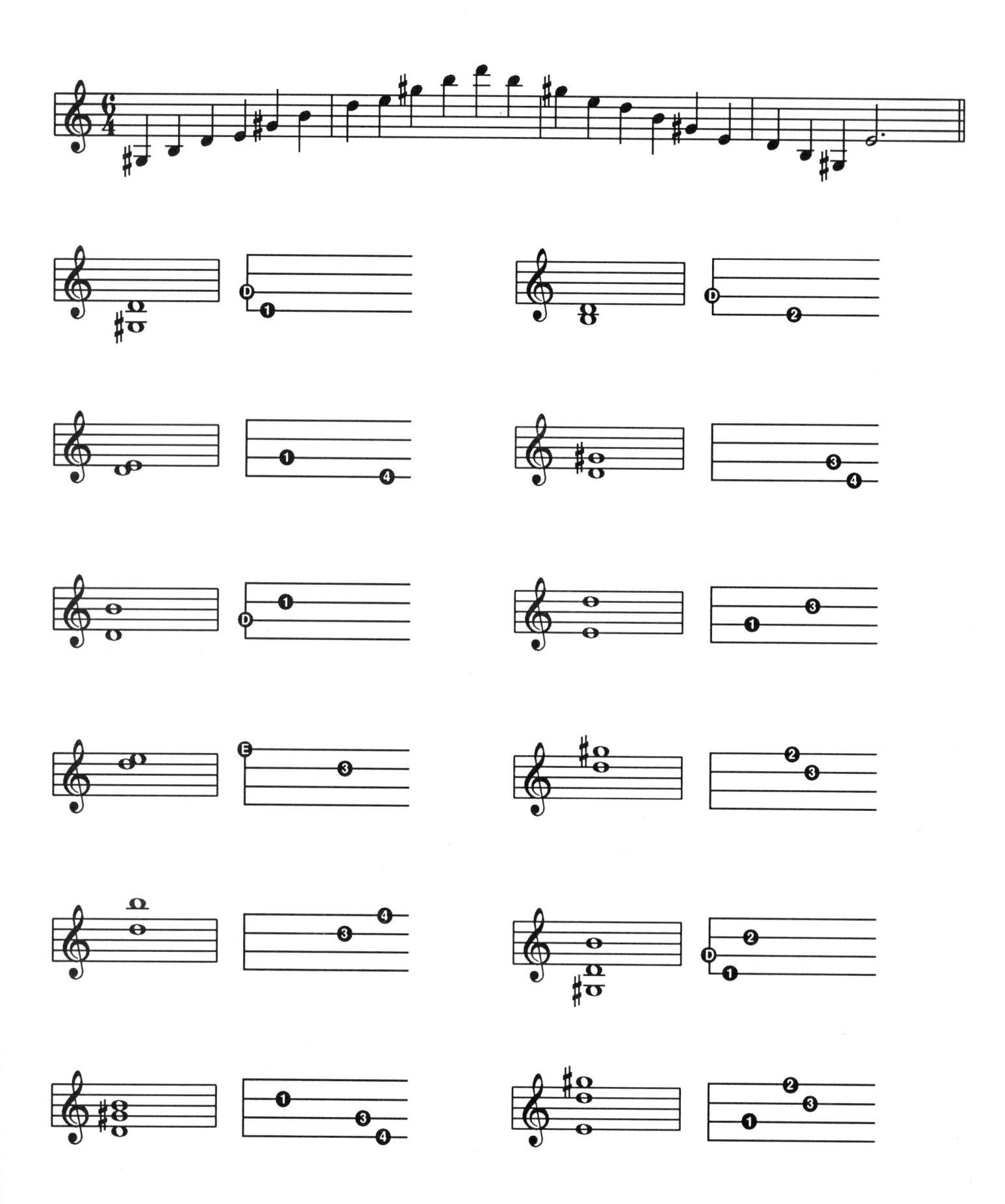

The F7 Chord

The notes in the F7 chord are F, A, C and E♭.

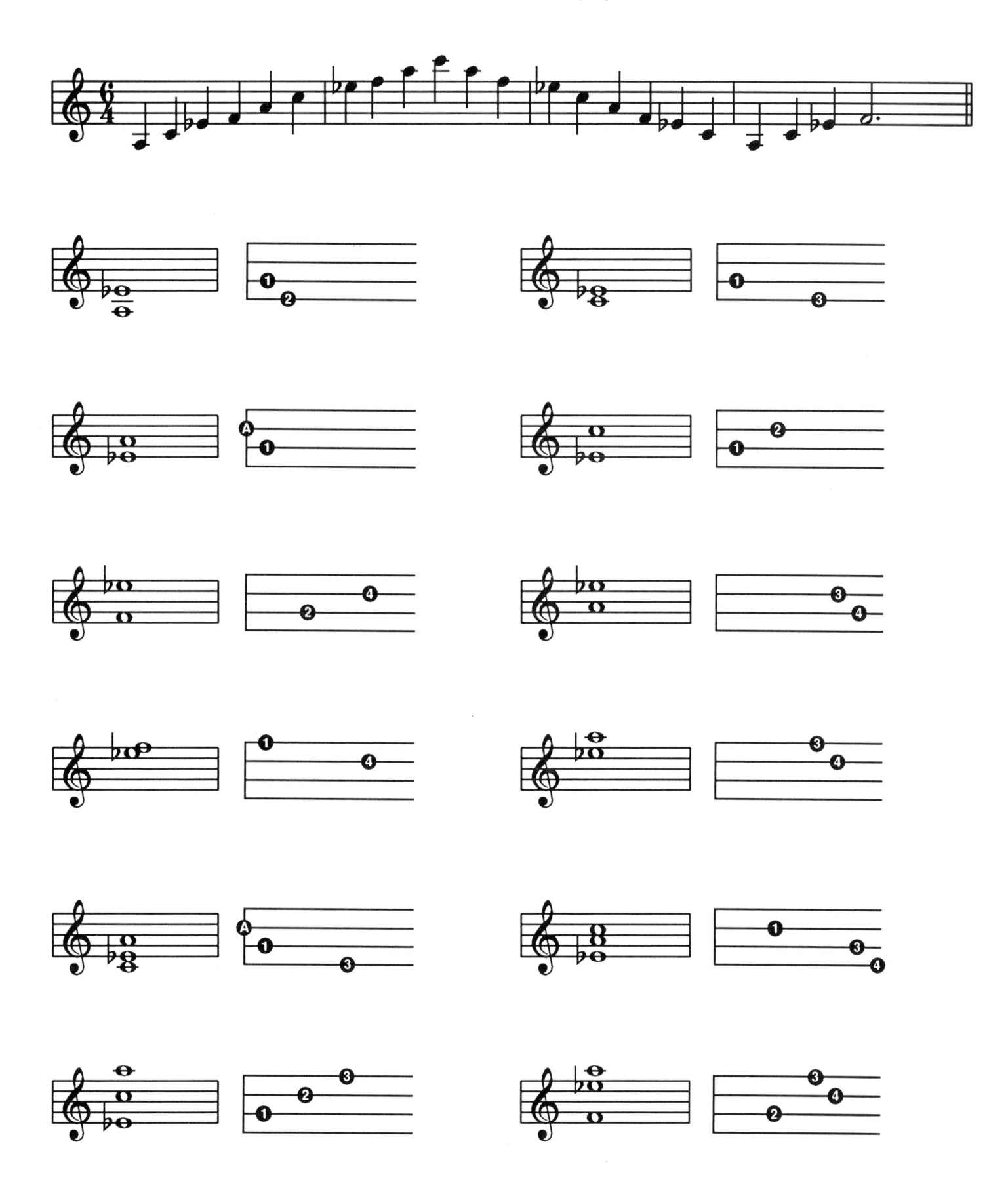

The F#7 Chord

The notes in the F#7 chord are F#, A#, C# and E.

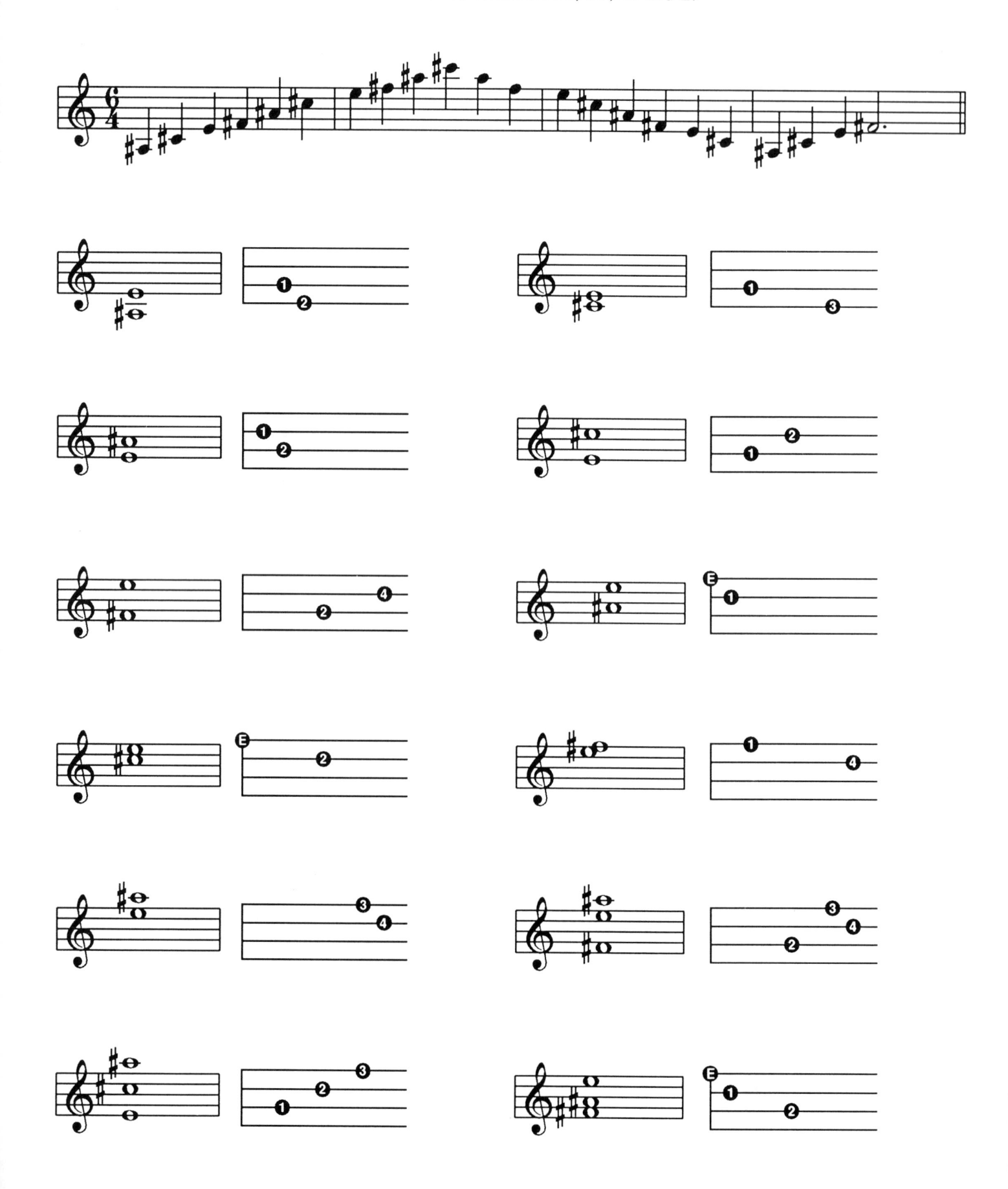

The G minor 7 Chord (Gm7)

The notes in the Gm7 chord are G, B♭, D and F.

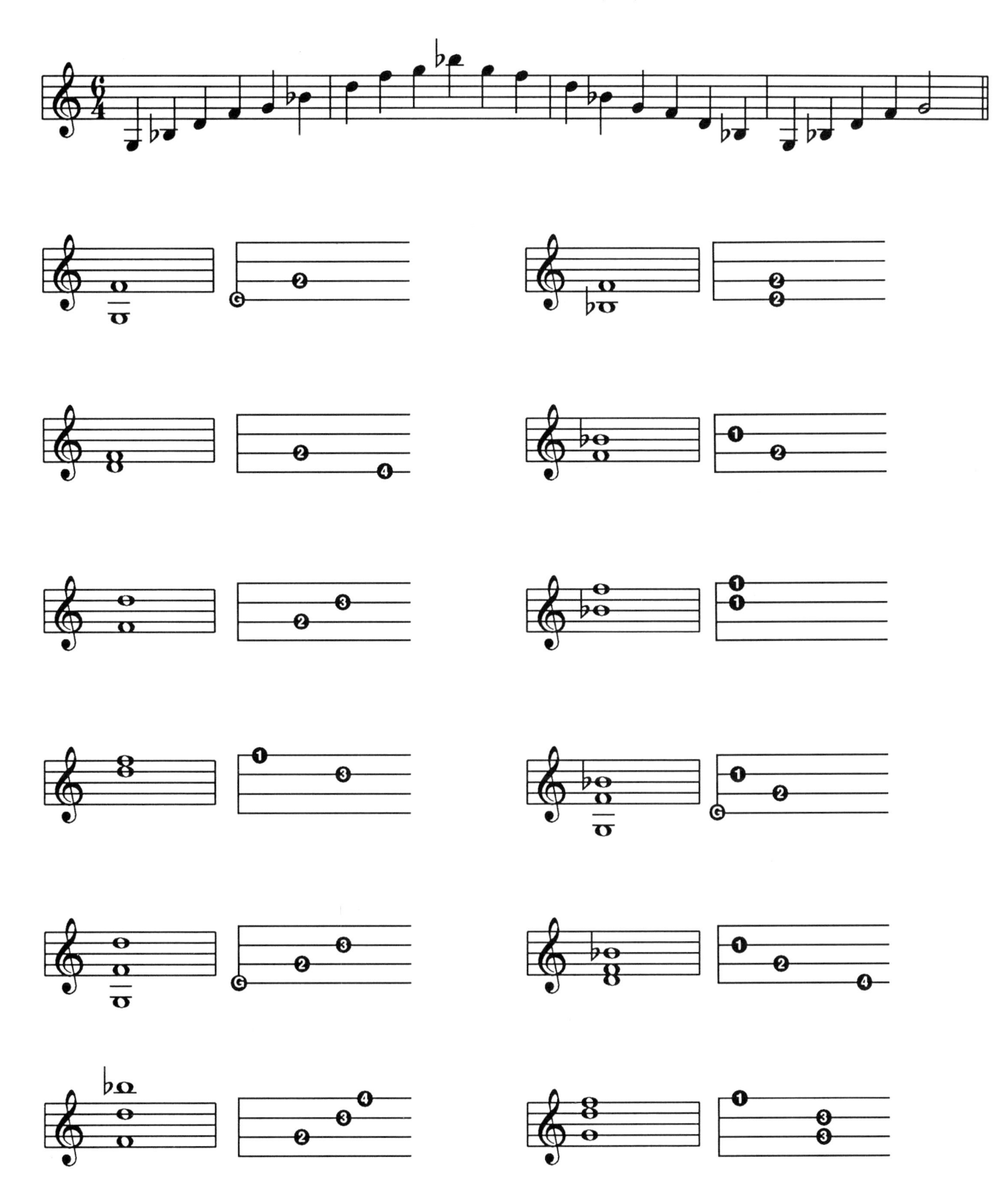

The G♯ minor 7 Chord (G♯m7)
The notes in the G♯m7 chord are G♯, B, D♯ and F♯.

The A minor 7 Chord (Am7)

The notes in the Am7 chord are A, C, E and G.

The B♭ minor 7 Chord (B♭m7)

The notes in the B♭m7 chord are B♭, D♭, F and A♭.

The B minor 7 Chord (Bm7)

The notes in the Bm7 chord are B, D, F# and A.

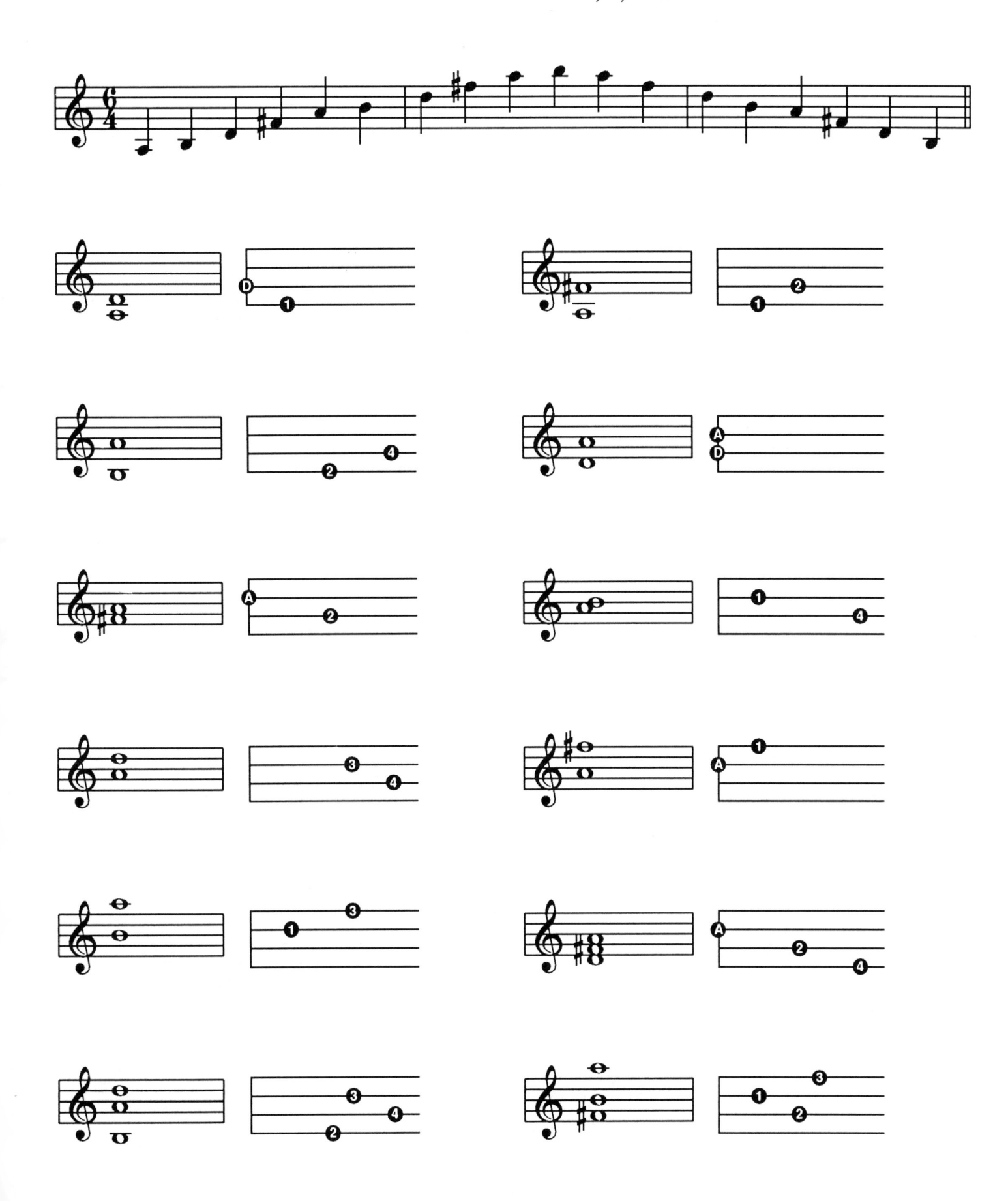

The C minor 7 Chord (Cm7)
The notes in the Cm7 chord are C, E♭, G and B♭.

The C♯ minor 7 Chord (C♯m7)
The notes in the C♯m7 chord are C♯, E, G♯ and B.

The D minor 7 Chord (Dm7)

The notes in the Dm7 chord are D, F, A and C.

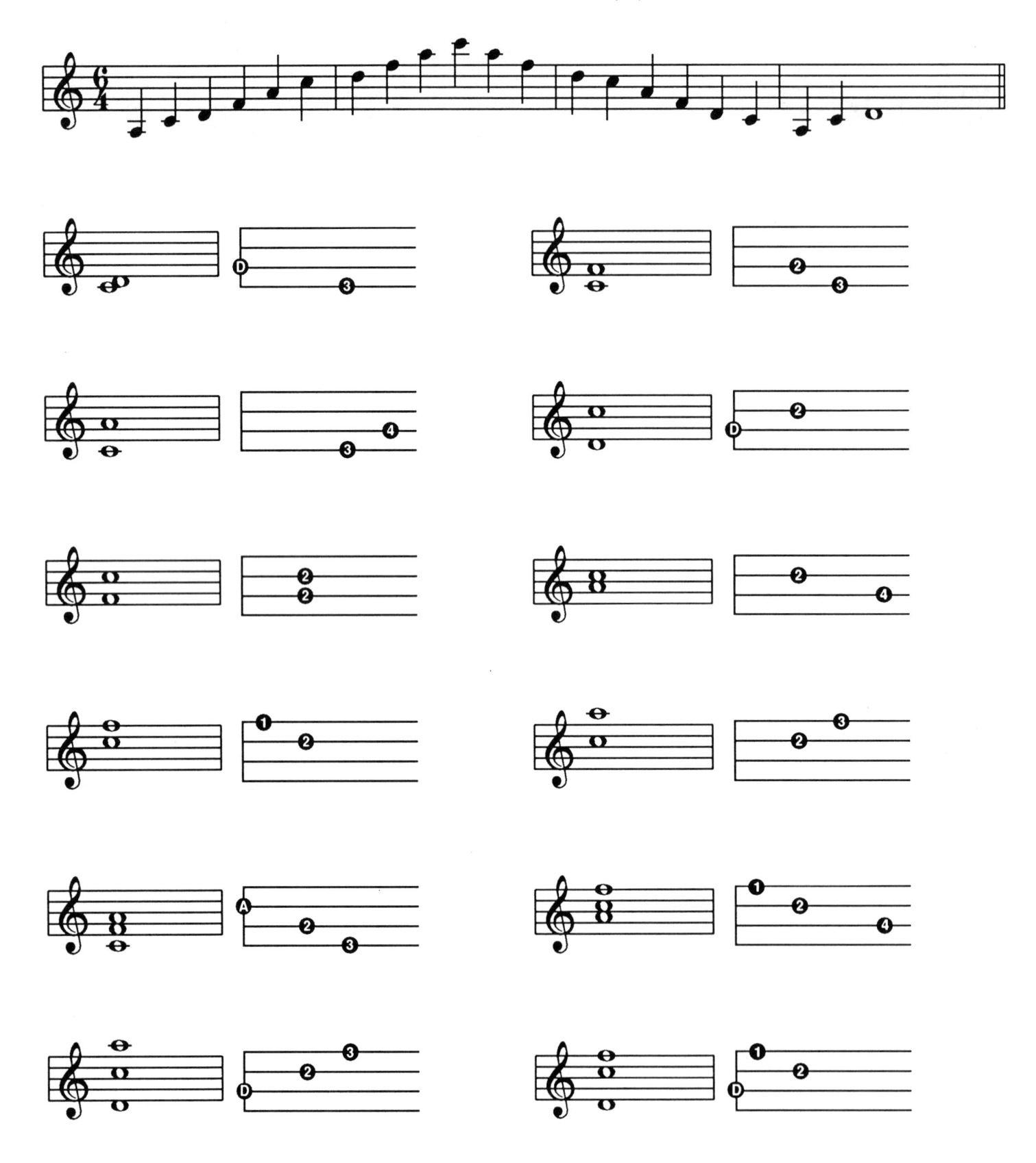

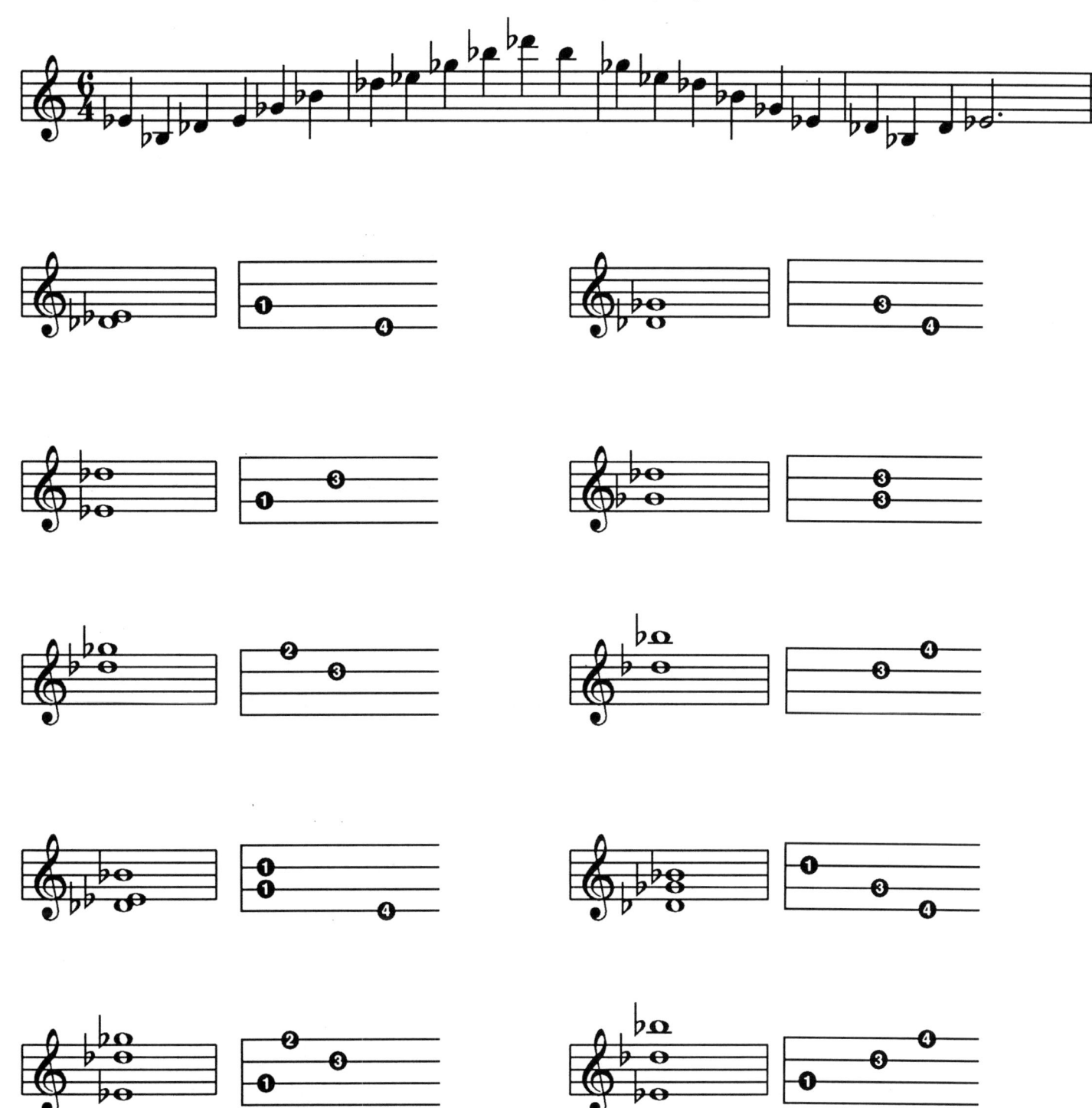

The E♭ minor 7 Chord (E♭m7)

The notes in the E♭m7 chord are E♭, G♭, B♭ and D♭.

The E minor 7 Chord (Em7)
The notes in the Em7 chord are E, G, B and D.

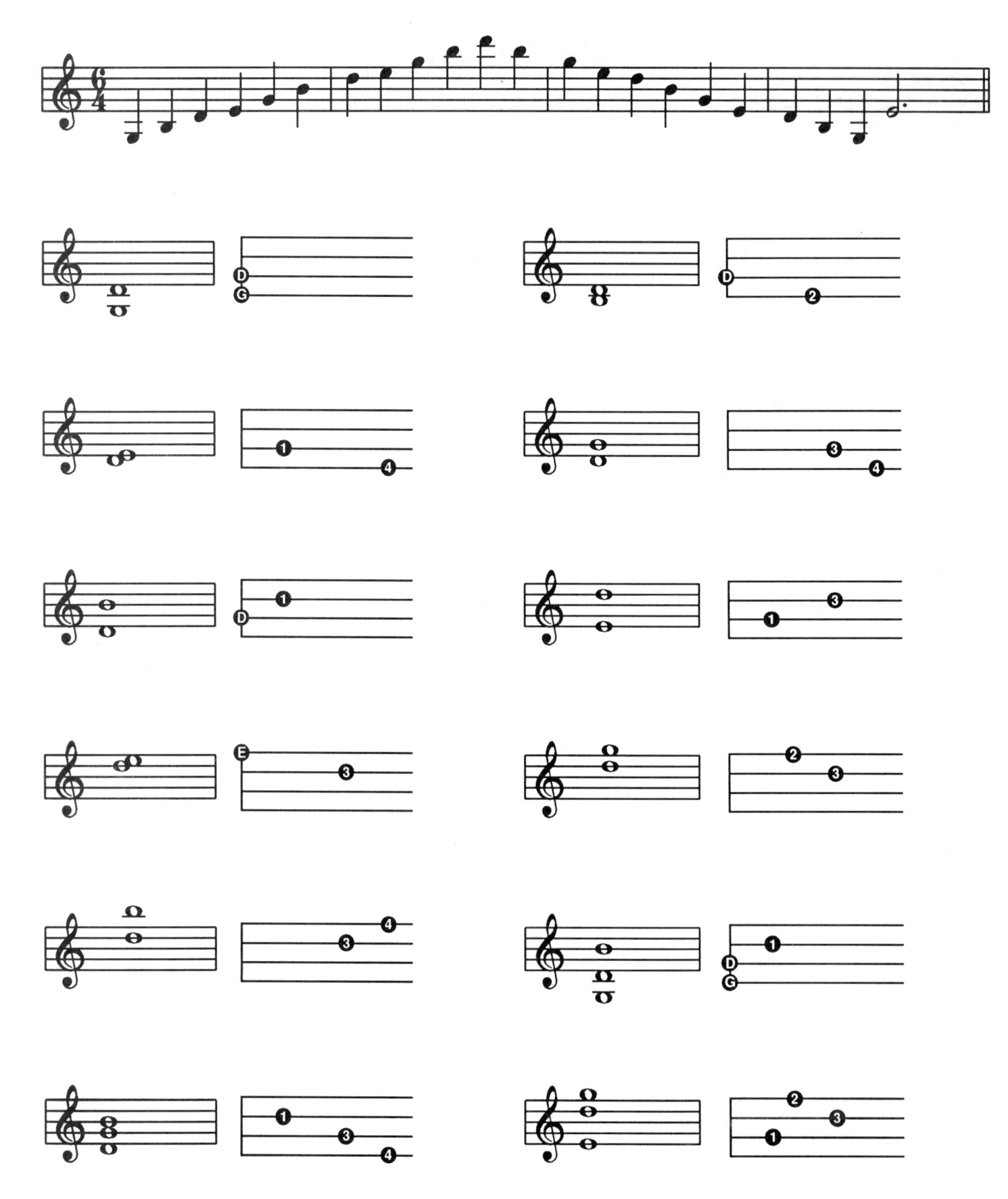

The F minor 7 Chord (Fm7)

The notes in the Fm7 chord are F, A♭, C and E♭.

The F♯ minor 7 Chord (F♯m7)

The notes in the F♯m7 chord are F♯, A, C♯ and E.

The G6 Chord

The notes in the G6 chord are G, B, D and F.

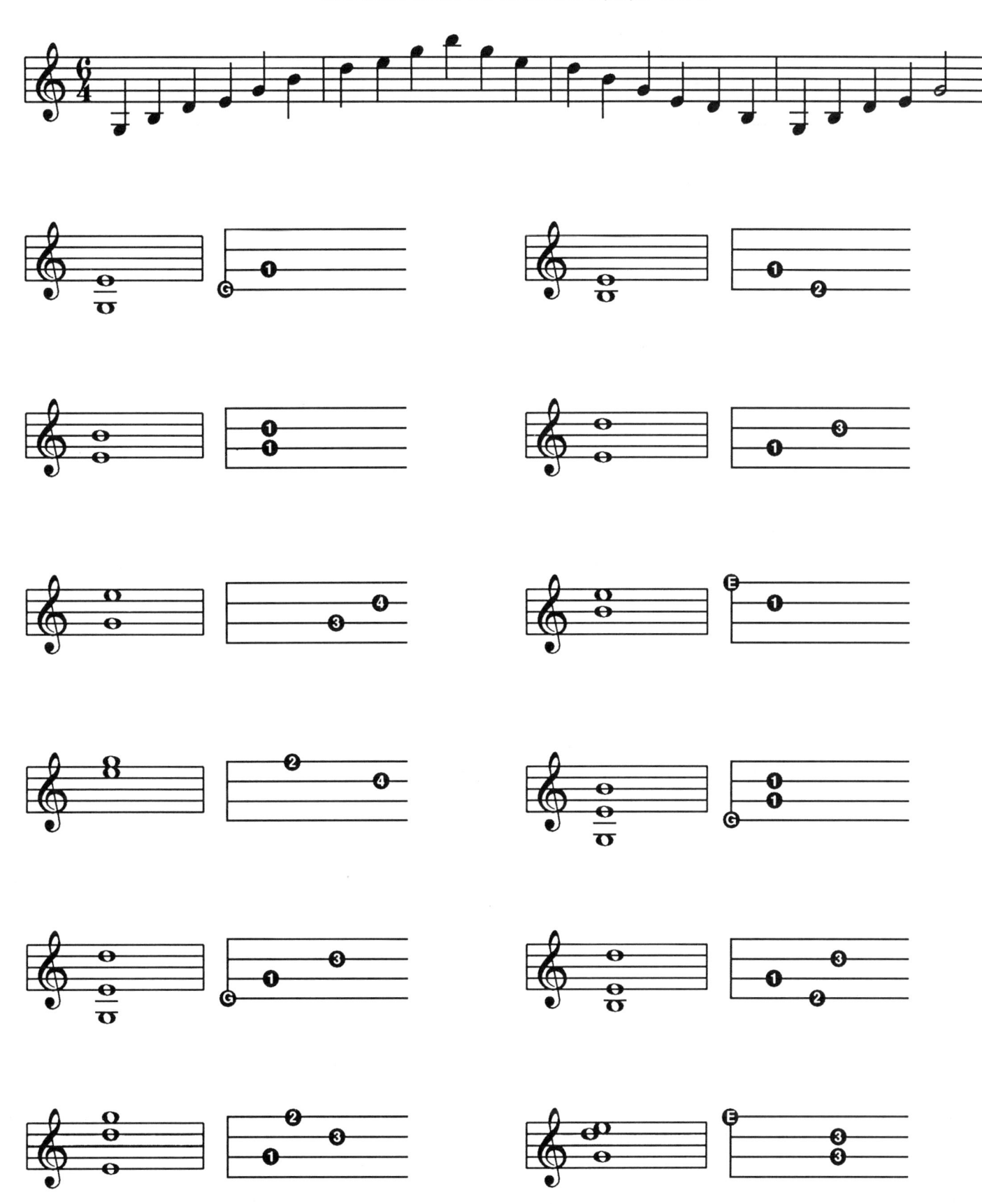

The A♭6 Chord

The notes in the A♭6 chord are A♭, C, E♭ and F.

The A6 Chord

The notes in the A6 chord are A, C#, E and F#.

The B♭6 Chord

The notes in the B♭6 chord are B♭, D, F and G.

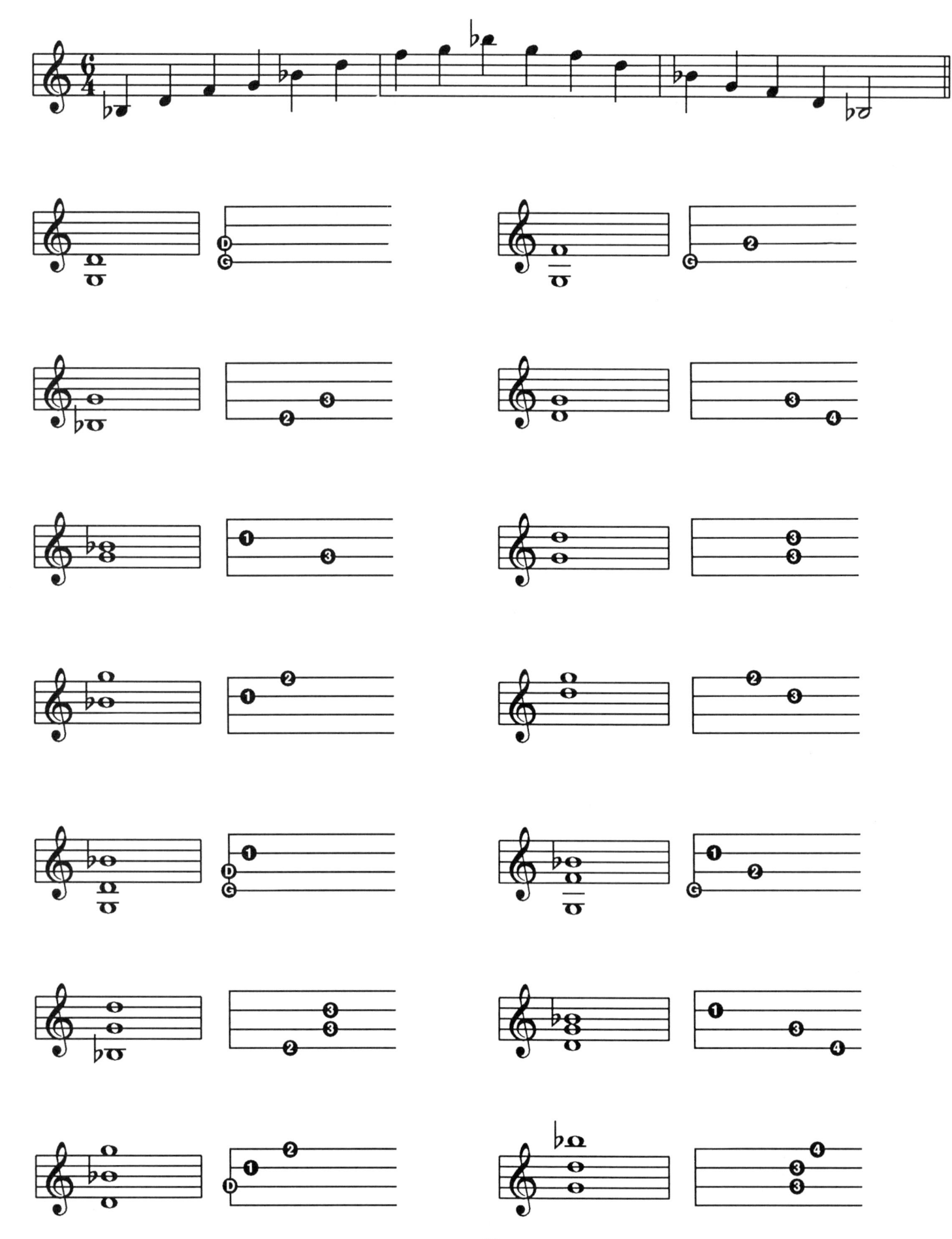

The B6 Chord

The notes in the B6 chord are B, D#, F# and G#.

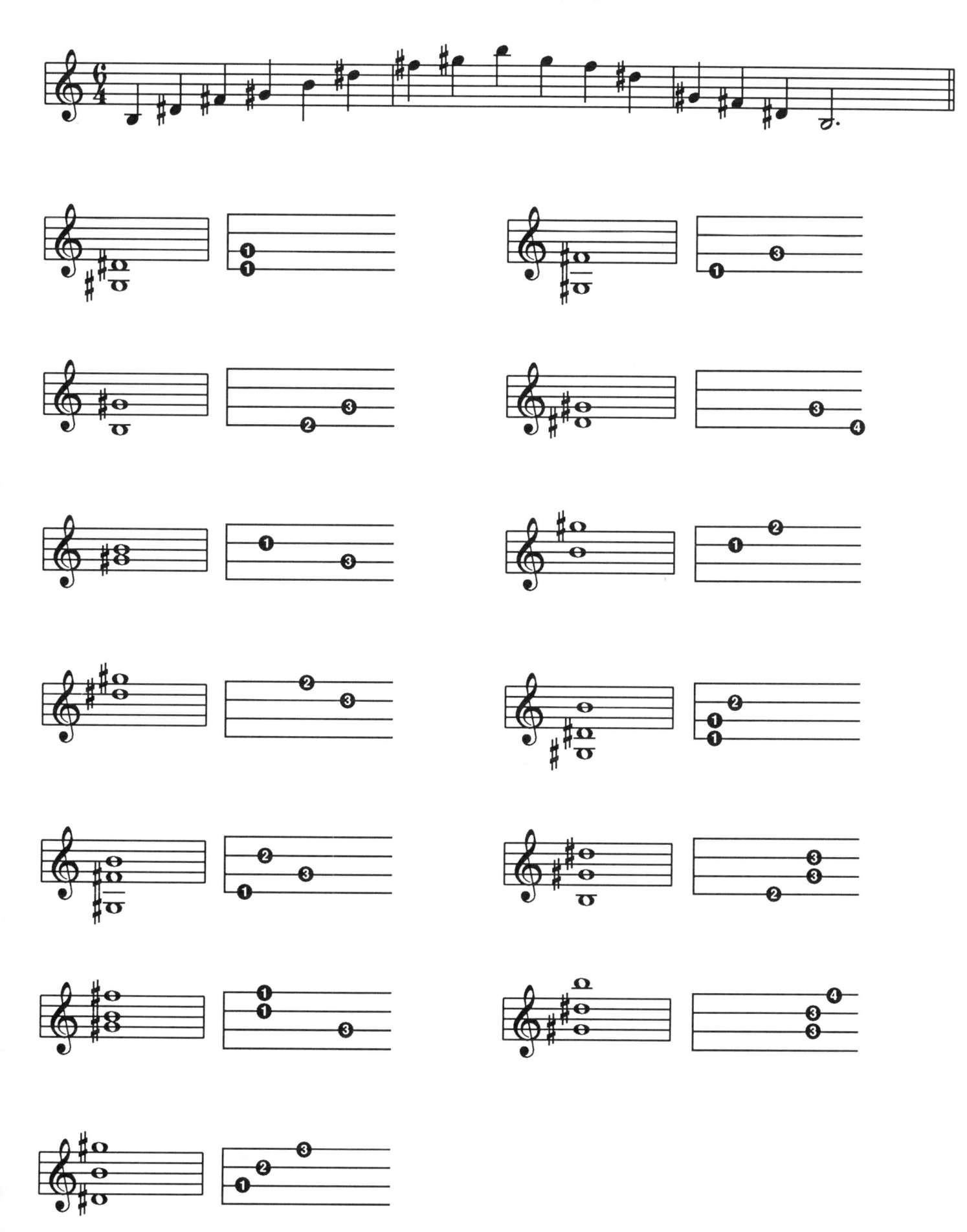

The C6 Chord

The notes in the C6 chord are C, E, G and A.

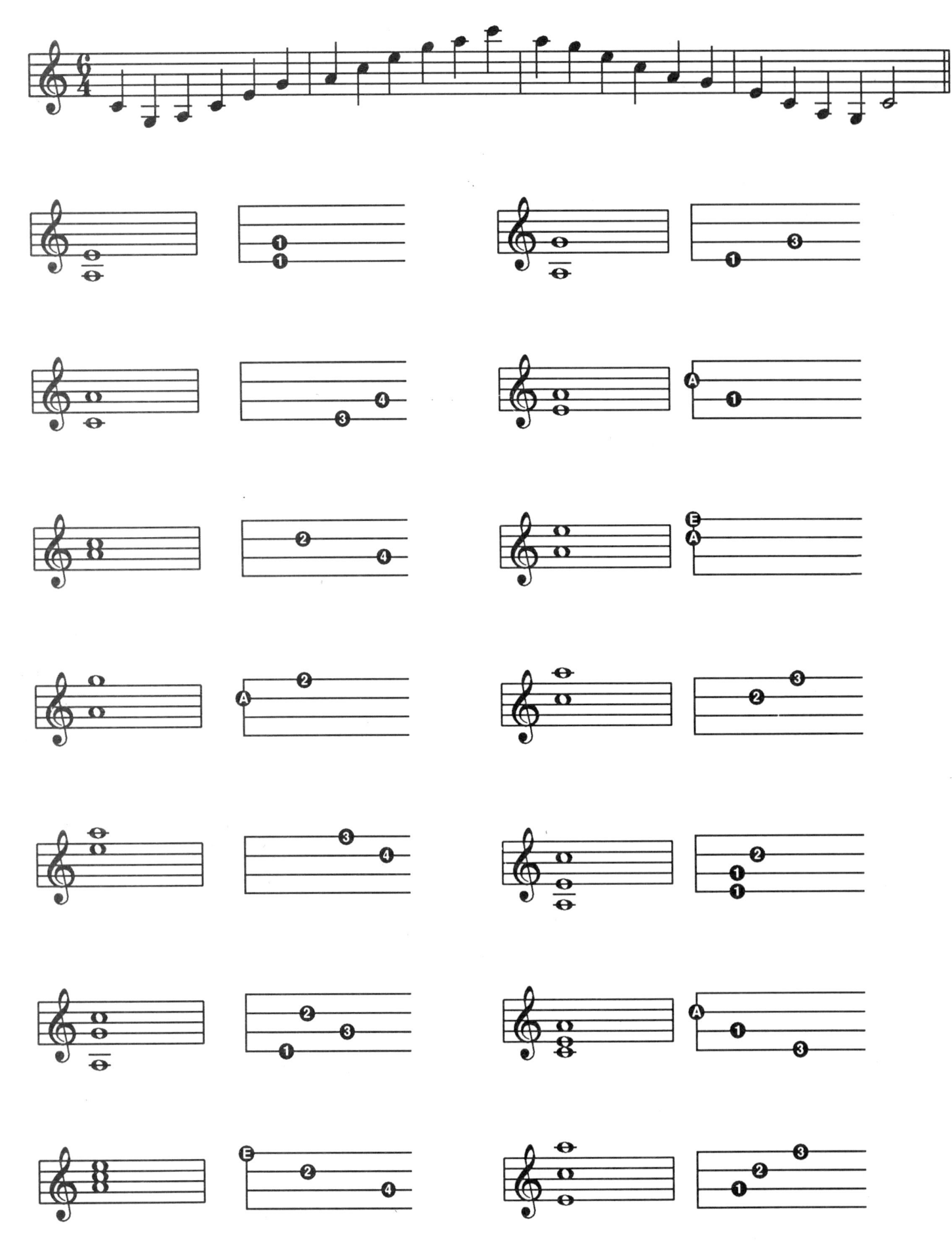

The C#6 Chord

The notes in the C#6 chord are C#, E#, G# and A#.

The D6 Chord

The notes in the D6 chord are D, F#, A and B.

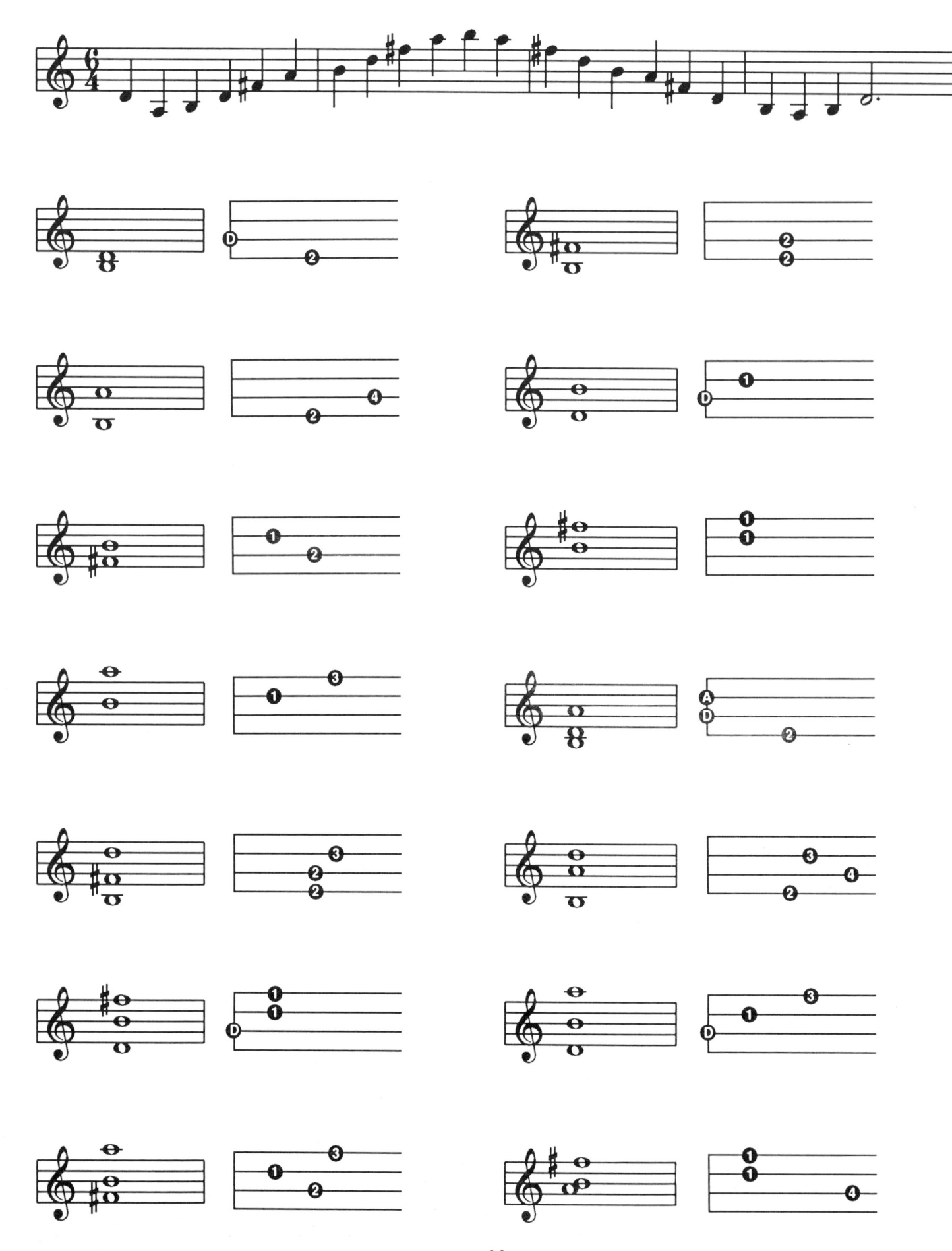

The E♭6 Chord

The notes in the E♭6 chord are E♭, G, B♭ and C.

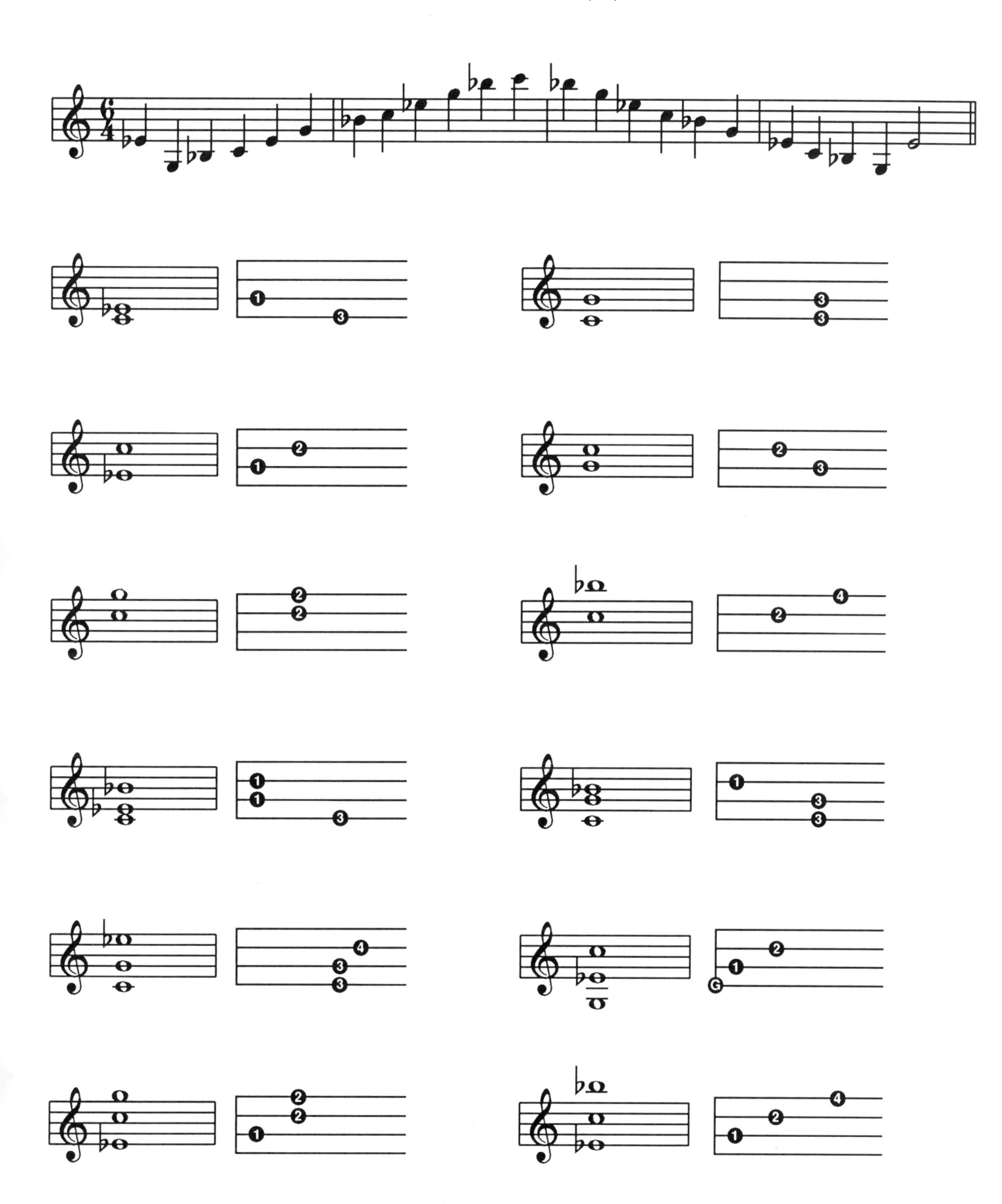

The E6 Chord

The notes in the E6 chord are E, G#, B and C#.

The F6 Chord

The notes in the F6 chord are F, A, C and D.

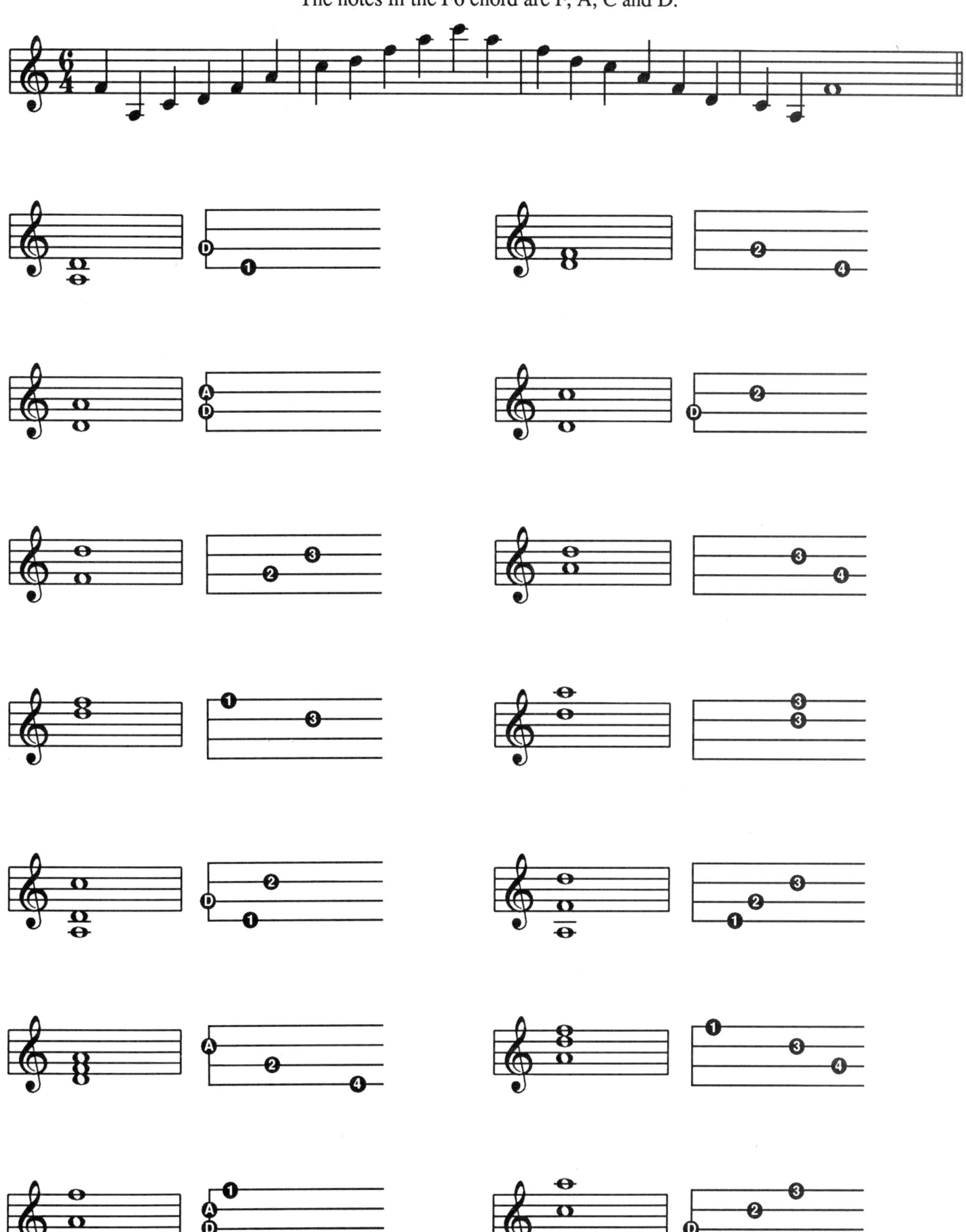

The F#6 Chord
The notes in the F#6 chord are F#, A#, C# and D#.

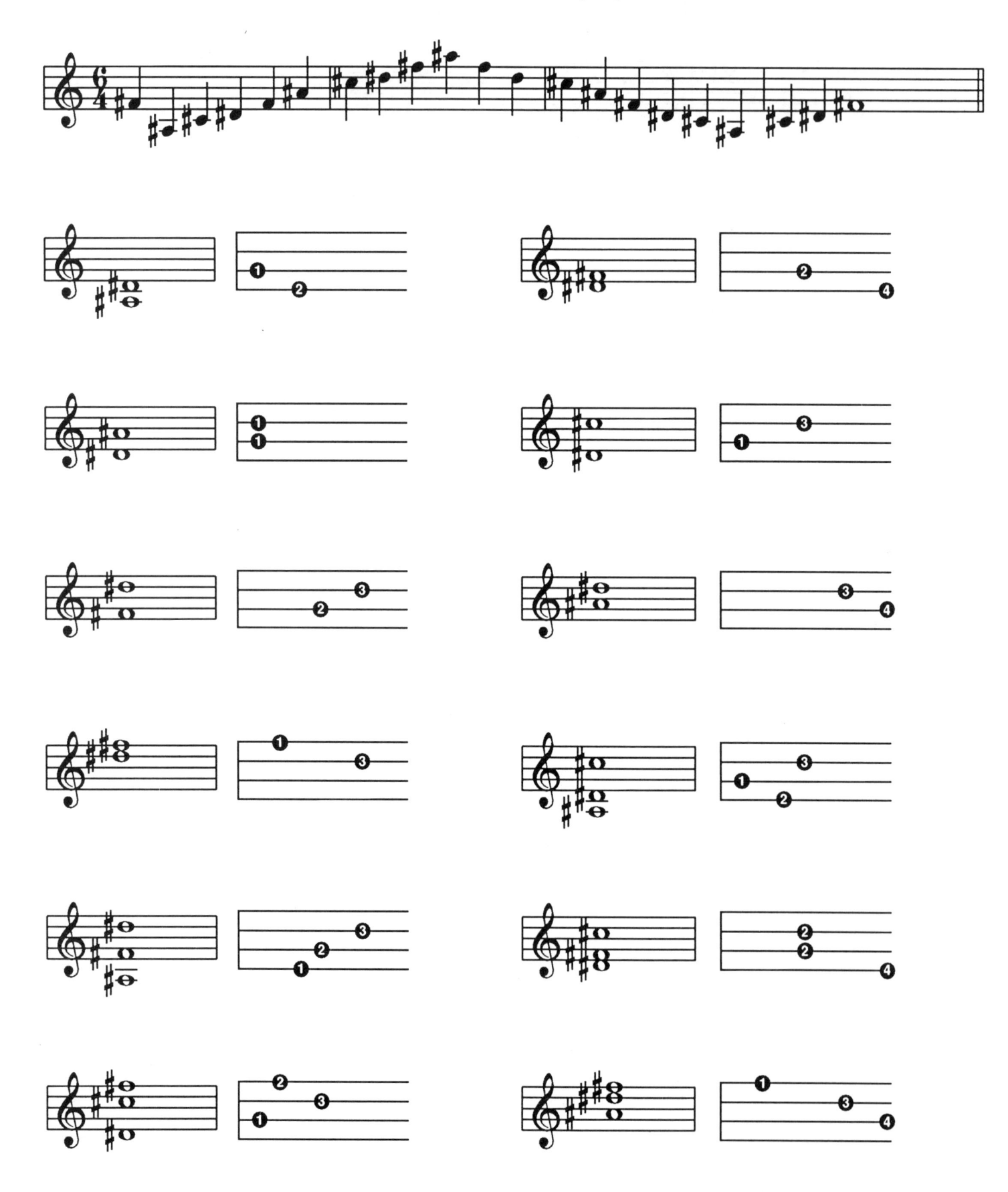